W9-BTC-869

The Bread Machine
Cookbook III

Donna Rathmell German

BRISTOL PUBLISHING ENTERPRISES, INC.
San Leandro, California

A Nitty Gritty® Cookbook

Printed in the United States of America.

ISBN 1-55867-048-3

Cover design: Frank Paredes
Cover photography: John Benson

CONTENTS

Thanks to Melody McKinley, Debbie Nicholson, Amy Peacock,
Rhonda Lechner and Mary Vollendorf for their testing
and to the many Marine Sentry guards and the midshipmen
at the U.S. Naval Academy for eating all the loaves of bread.

A special thanks to Megan Pyle, Shannon Mulloy, my husband, Lee,
and my special helpers, Rachel (4), Katie (2)) and Helen (1).
They all kept me going with their support, help and encouragement.

ABOUT BREAD MACHINES

The recipes in all of my books are continuously tested and updated as new bread machines are introduced. Because there are so many machine makes and models, I do not describe each. It is important for you to become familiar with the owner's manual and/or the recipe book that came with your machine. There are a few pieces of information which you must determine about your particular machine in order to know how to make any recipe.

INGREDIENT ORDER

Manufacterers indicate the order in which the ingredients should be put into the pan. In 9 out of 10 machines, you start with the liquid; in the other 10%, you begin with yeast and then flour. For example, DAK, Welbilt and Citizen machines call for yeast and flour first, so the liquid will not leak through the hole in the bottom of the pan. For such machines, reverse the order of ingredients in my recipes, beginning with yeast. *The really important point is that the liquid ingredients are kept away from the yeast until the machine starts.*

RECIPE SIZE FOR YOUR MACHINE

You must determine the size of your machine. Machines are sold as 1 lb., 1½ lb. and 2 lb. machines. This may be somewhat confusing, because the weight of a loaf will vary depending on the ingredients used. If your machine manual does not specify the size of the machine given by weight of loaf, it is easily determined by looking at the amount of flour in the recipes that come with the machine.

In general, **1 lb. machines** use 2 to 2¼ cups of bread flour or 2 to 2¾ total cups of combined flours such as bread flour, whole wheat, rye, oats, corn, etc. For whole grain flours, 2½ to 3 cups can be used. *If you have a 1 lb. machine, you will be using the Small recipe*, depending on the ingredients and flour equivalents.

A **1½ lb. machine** uses 3 cups of bread flour or 3½ to 4 total cups of combined flours such as bread flour, whole wheat, rye, oats, corn, etc. Up to 5 cups of whole grain flours can be used in most 1½ lb. machines without fear of overflows. *Most 1½ lb. machines will take the Medium recipe* depending on the ingredients and flour equivalents.

A full **2 lb. machine** can use up to 4 cups of bread flour, although I find that 3½ cups usually results in a nice loaf of bread at or just over the lip of the pan. A total of 4 or 5 cups of combination flours (bread with whole wheat, oats, rye, corn, etc.) can easily be used and up to 6 cups of whole grain flours. Some machines are being introduced as 2 lb. machines, but the size of the pan is the same as the 1½ lb. pan, and therefore must use Medium size recipes. It is necessary to keep an eye on the dough to prevent overflows. *A full 2 lb. machine will use the Large recipe.*

After years of working with all machine makes and models, I can assure you that there are some variables and individual preferences in the sizes of recipes used. For example, one friend with a 1 lb. machine (2 cups of flour, generally) makes Medium recipes, which would seem too large for her machine. My father, however, has a large machine and consistently uses recipes with just 2 cups of flour; in the identical machine I use 3½ cups of flour with success.

Unlike any other bread machine cookbook on the market, I give you three different sizes for each recipe. If a recipe is too large, next time use a smaller size. With the exception of National/Panasonic 65 model machines, all machines can make a smaller size recipe.

A few words about pushing the maximum flour capacity of your bread machine:

If at any time it sounds like the machine is struggling with a large amount of flour, add a tablespoon or two of water (or more if necessary) to soften the dough. If the machine is struggling, it could cause damage to the motor.

The sides of the machine may require scraping to help get all ingredients to the kneading paddle. Once the dough has formed a ball it will do just fine and can be left. If it has taken the machine a long time to knead the ingredients into a ball, you can stop the machine and start it over from the beginning, giving the dough a little longer knead.

One of the main concerns about using too much flour is overflowing the sides of the pan. Usually you will end up with a mushroom — the dough may cook onto the lid of the pan or may not cook properly at the top. The real mess, however, is when the dough spills down the sides of the pan into the inside of the machine and onto the heating elements. Cleanup is a messy, time-consuming chore (I've done it often in testing). It is difficult to remove all dough from the heating elements, but it burns off the next time the machine is used.

It is wise to check the dough during the second rise. If it looks too high, use a bamboo skewer (or something similar) and pierce deep into the dough to deflate it. Do not use metal objects which could scratch the pan. If you have absolutely used the wrong size recipe and it is starting to overflow, remove a portion of the dough. This enables you to at least salvage something!

BREAD MACHINE FEATURES

CYCLES

Initially, all recipes were tested using only the basic white cycles. Later testing has indicated that the DAK and Welbilt ABM 100 machines perform more consistently on the sweet cycle.

The same cycle may have many names. A sweet cycle may be called *sweet*, *mix* or *fruit and nut*. Most machines now have whole wheat cycles, but any machine can make whole wheat bread on the regular (basic, white) cycle.

You may have a specific cycle with a "beep" for adding raisins, a beep on all cycles or no beep at all. In any case, add ingredients at the beginning of the second kneading, or during the rest between kneadings. If you have only one kneading, add extra ingredients as soon as dough has formed a ball, about 5 to 10 minutes into the kneading.

Basic white bread cycles may have one or two main kneadings depending on the machine. Some machines have only a basic cycle which is used for all breads.

Sweet cycles should be used with recipes containing 2 tbs. or more sugar and/or fat (butter, margarine or oil). These cycles may have a longer rising time. The baking temperature is lower than the basic cycles for the higher sugar content of the breads.

French bread cycles may or may not have a longer rising time but all have a higher baking temperature to crisp the crust.

Raisin cycles have a beep to indicate when to add raisins, nuts or other similar ingredients. Generally the beep is about 5 minutes before the end of the kneading. The cycles may have a lower baking temperature (like the sweet cycle).

Whole grain cycles generally have longer kneadings and longer risings.

Dough cycles include the initial kneading of the dough and one rise, after which time the dough is removed from the machine, shaped, allowed to rise and baked in a conventional oven. This is the cycle used for bagels, rolls, pizza crust, etc. For best results, DAK, Welbilt ABM 100 and Citizen machines should be stopped after the first rise and before the second kneading.

OTHER FEATURES

Timers enable the user to place ingredients in the machine and to tell the machine when to have the bread ready, whether at 6:00 in the evening or 7:00 in the morning. Most timers have a 12- or 13-hour limit. With the exception of the Seiko 211 and the Welbilt ABM 600, all machines have a timer feature. Recipes that contain ingredients that may spoil if unrefrigerated (eggs, milk, cheese, etc.) should not be used with the timer.

Preheating periods are found on only a few machines. Basically the machine heats all ingredients to the proper temperature prior to starting the kneading period.

Crust controls are usually buttons pushed when you start your machine, such as basic white, light setting. Some machines such as the DAK/Welbilt 100 machines, have a control knob. The controls shorten or lengther the baking time by about 5 minutes.

Power outage protecion prevents a short (usually 10 minutes or less) loss of electricity from stopping the entire machine process. If this is not included with your machine and you have a loss of electricity, simply remove the dough and finish baking the bread conventionally.

Viewing windows are a nice feature if you like to frequently check the process of your bread. It is always a good idea to check the dough about 5 minutes into the initial kneading to make sure that all is going well. If you don't have a viewing window, simply open the lid long enough to check the dough. Don't leave the machine open for long periods of time.

Cooling/warming periods are found in many machines to either start cooling the bread or to keep it warm until it is removed from the machine. This is to prevent the bread from becoming soggy and wet if not removed as soon as the baking is completed.

HELPFUL HINTS

Many machine manufacterers recommend bringing the liquid to lukewarm temperature. If your machine does not have a preheating cycle, a simple rule of thumb is to have the temperature of the liquid similar to a baby's bottle — warm but comfortable on the inside of your wrist. If removing something directly from the refrigerator, I generally "nuke" it in the microwave for one minute. Keep in mind that ingredients used on a machine's timer cycle will not be lukewarm when the kneading starts. I have often used ingredients at room temperature and had good results.

Butter is okay to use straight from the refrigerator, and it's easier to cut into the measured tablespoons. I simply take the measured amount and then cut that into smaller pieces — maybe quarters. Just make sure that the butter does not come in direct contact with the yeast.

Ingredients such as rice, cheese or potatoes should be lightly packed into the measuring cup.

Recipes that use fruits or vegetables as a source of liquid should be checked about 3 to 5 minutes into the initial kneading. One fruit or vegetable may have a different moisture content than another and, therefore, the dough may need additional water or flour.

SUBSTITUTIONS AND MEASUREMENTS

Many people have asked about ingredients which may be substituted for one another or added to a recipe. Hopefully the following information and guidelines will help give you some ideas to use as a springboard. I enjoy walking the aisles of grocery stores, kitchen or gourmet stores and browsing through mail order catalogs looking for new and interesting food items to add to bread.

Questions are received about adding various seeds, nuts or dried fruits to recipes which are already favorites. One aspect about the bread machines is that they make experimenting so easy. For the most part, the answer is to go ahead and make your additions.

Please note that many of the additions which are listed together may also serve as substitutions for each other.

ADDITIONS

SEEDS can be added to recipes to taste - amounts can range anywhere from half a teaspoon to one tablespoon. Toasted pumpkin seeds and sunflower seeds seem more like nuts and are included in the nut section. Nuts and seeds may be added to the top of the loaf just prior to baking. Be careful not to spill any down the side of the pan into the machine where they may burn.

(anise, caraway, coriander, dill, fennel, flax, poppy, sesame)

DRIED FRUITS sometimes cause problems. Keep in mind that some machines have difficulty baking loaves which have too many dried or fresh fruits. For this reason, I generally recommend adding between ¼ to ⅓ cup for small size loaf, ⅓ to ½ cup for medium and ½ to ⅔ cup for a large loaf. Experiment to determine which is best for you.

(apple, apricots, blueberries, cherries, cranberries, dried fruit mix, raisins)

NUTS, ground or chopped nuts, can be added in amounts ranging from ¼ to ⅓ cup for a small loaf, ⅓ to ½ cup for medium and ½ to ⅔ for large loaves.

(almonds, brazil, cashew, hazelnuts, macadamia, mixed, peanuts, sunflower or pumpkin seeds, walnuts, pecans, pistachios)

INGREDIENTS AND SUBSTITUTIONS

YEAST is the leavening agent used in all of these recipes. When bread machines were first introduced, the only yeast readily available was the expensive active yeast found in three packets. Now you can find less expensive jars of yeast in just about any grocery store. In recent testing, fast-acting yeast (also called bread machine, rapid, instant or quick yeast) consistently resulted in higher rising loaves compared to those made with regular dry active yeast. Fast-acting yeast can be used on either the regular or quick/turbo cycle. Testing is done on these recipes using a fast yeast in the amount listed. Active yeast may be used in the same amounts or slightly "heaped" and should be used on the regular cycle.

Yeast responds to ambient temperatures. It may be necessary to increase yeast in colder weather or to decrease it in very hot temperatures. Too much yeast may cause air pockets or air bubbles. Compressed (cake) yeast is not recommended for use in bread machines.

SALT is one of those necessary "evils" of bread baking. Salt restricts the growth of the yeast and hence the rising of the dough. Without salt, the dough will rise too quickly or too high and then collapse. I have been experimenting with decreasing the salt amounts as much as possible and have successfully used ⅛ tsp. in the small and medium size recipes and ¼ tsp. in the large. For people on a salt-restricted diet, ground dehydrated vegetable flakes (food processor or blender) may be substituted. Check your health food store for a vegetable salt which is used in a 3:1 ratio. That is, if your recipe calls for ⅓ tsp. of salt, use 1 tsp. of vegetable salt (see page 16 for a conversion chart).

SUGAR or sweeteners are required in bread baking to feed the yeast which enables the dough to rise.

Granulated sugars which may be substituted on a basic 1:1 ratio include: brown sugar; refined white sugar; maple sugar (maple syrup which has been cooked slowly until dried into granules); date sugar (finely ground dried dates); sucanet (evaporated sugar cane juice — the only process which it has undergone is the removal of the water. Sucanet contains more nutrients than brown or turbinado sugars); turbinado sugar ("raw" sugar which is less refined than white sugar, that is, not subject to chemical whitening).

Fructose, a natural fruit sugar, is sweeter than sugar so less is needed (rule of thumb is 1/3 the sugar amount).

Liquid sweeteners which may be substituted on a 1:1 basis include: honey; molasses; barley malt syrup; fruit syrups; maple syrup; and rice syrup. Liquid sweeteners and granulated sweeteners are interchangeable; however, liquid amounts may require adjusting. For example, if a recipe calls for 1 tbs. of sugar and you would prefer to use honey, you may need to delete 1 tbs. of the liquid.

BUTTER, MARGARINE, VEGETABLE AND NUT OILS are all interchangeable on a 1:1 basis. Note that any of my recipes which use honey, molasses or a syrup generally call for an oil instead of butter or margarine. The reason for this is quite simple: I measure my oil and then use the same spoon for the honey which then slides out of the spoon quite easily.

Applesauce may replace fat, tablespoon for tablespoon, but is not to exceed 1 tbs. per cup of flour. If using more applesauce than the amount of butter or oil called for, the liquid should be reduced proportionately.

Fruit juice concentrates, such as frozen apple or orange juice which is found in the grocery store, may replace fat. The concentrate should be thawed but not diluted. Many other fruit juice concentrates are available through a health food store. Each adds a very slight flavoring to the bread which may not even be noticed by many. I started using this as a substitute for sugar or other sweetener but I found that, due to the pectin (a natural substance in fruit), the concentrates better replaced the fat.

Miso is a fermented soybean paste which can replace fat. However, miso contains salt already so OMIT salt from the recipe. Purcase miso at a health food store.

MILK - If a recipe calls for milk but you have an allergy or you would like to use the timer cycle, you may simply substitute water or juice on a cup-for-cup basis. Nutrition may be boosted by adding dry milk powder in with the flour and other dry ingredients, if desired. Try adding 1 tbs. per every cup of flour used. As this is a small percentage of the total dry ingredients no changes are necessary to the liquid or dry amounts. Likewise, if dried milk powder is called for, it may simply be omitted.

BUTTERMILK is produced by adding bacterial cultures (like yogurt) called lactobacilli to either lowfat or skim milk. The milk is allowed to sit at room temperature for approximately 24 hours — similar to a sourdough culture. It is then refrigerated which slows down the bacterial action. Buttermilk is usually low in calories and fat, and when added to bread, results in a light, high rising and tender bread. Buttermilk requires baking soda to be used to offset the slight acidity. Substitutes for buttermilk are yogurt, sour cream, or 1 tbs. vinegar or lemon juice in bottom of cup with milk added to equal 1 cup.

EGGS add richness, flavor and color to breads. If eggs are called for in a recipe, and you prefer not to use them, just add whatever liquid you are using to compensate for the loss of the egg. A general rule of thumb is ¼ cup of liquid for each whole egg. You should watch the dough and add the liquid as it is kneading until a round ball of dough is formed. Egg substitutes are available in grocery stores: ¼ cup equals one egg. Dry egg powder is available: 1½ tsp. plus 2 tbs. water equals one egg. Egg powder may be purchased at a health food store or by mail (see *Sources*, page 183).

VITAL GLUTEN is listed as an optional ingredient in some recipes. Found at a health food store or via mail order catalogs (see Sources, page 183), vital gluten is added to recipes in a range from 1 tsp. to 1 tbs. per cup of flour used. Gluten is a natural protein contained in wheat and some other grains. The gluten in the flour and the yeast combine during kneading to release a gas which causes the dough to rise. Grains which have a small amount of gluten, such as corn, oats, and rye, will not rise as high as a loaf of all-wheat flour. For this reason, vital gluten may be added to assist in the rising of the dough. Substitutes for vital gluten would be xanthum gum or guar gum which are also available at health food stores or through mail order catalogs. Please note that vital gluten is not the same thing as gluten flour, which is a mix of approximately 50% gluten and 50% wheat flour. Vital gluten is the actual gluten protein which has been washed out of the flour and is used in small amounts.

OATS and WHEAT FLAKES are very similar in appearance and may be used interchangeably. Both are made by rolling the oat groat or wheat kernel; hence they may also be found as rolled oats or wheat. The most commonly known rolled oats are the Quaker oats found at grocery stores. The difference between instant or quick cooking oats and "old-fashioned" oats is the thickness; both are acceptable in bread baking.

STEEL CUT OATS, also known as Scotch or Irish oats, are oat groats which have been dried and cut.

CRACKED WHEAT, sold as a packaged cereal or in bulk at health food stores, are wheat kernels which have been cut. It is necessary to soak cracked wheat in liquid for at least one hour prior to using. I generally measure whatever liquid will be used in the recipe and soak the measured cracked wheat right in it. This can be done right in most machines if using the timer cycle and liquid is the first ingredient called for in the pan. If your machine calls for the liquids last (Welbilt and DAK) or the machine kneads the ingredients when the machine's timer cycle is turned on (National/Panasonic), I recommend soaking the cracked wheat right in the measuring cup of liquid. Wheat bulgur may be substituted for the cracked wheat, but does not need soaking, so should be placed in the machine along with the dry ingredients. Some adjustment to the liquid amounts may be necessary.

WHIPPING CREAM is also known as heavy cream and may be substituted with evaporated skim milk if watching calories.

CREAM CHEESE may be replaced with yogurt cheese which is extremely easy to make. Use a plain low or nonfat yogurt which does not have any gelatin in it (I use Dannon Non Fat). Put a coffee filter inside a small colander and put a cup or two of the yogurt in the filtered colander. Place the colander over a bowl so the whey (the thin liquid) can drain into it and place both in the refrigerator for a few hours. The whey will drip out of the yogurt leaving it with a consistency similar to cream cheese. The whey may simply be discarded. This yogurt cheese may be substituted for both cream cheese and sour cream and has very few calories.

Measurement equivalents:

As the recipes are all provided in three different sizes to compensate for each machine's capacity; some measurements may not be as familiar to you as the normal standbys. To make this easy for you, I have broken down some information which may be helpful.

⅓ tsp.   = heaping ¼ tsp.
⅔ tsp.   = heaping ½ tsp. or
              scant ¾ tsp.
1 tsp.   = ⅓ tbs.
1½ tsp. = ½ tbs.
3 tsp.   = 1 tbs.

4 tsp.   = 1⅓ tbs.
⅓ tbs.   = 1 tsp.
½ tbs.   = 1½ tsp.
1 tbs.   = 3 tsp.
1⅓ tbs. = 4 tsp. or 1 tbs. plus 1 tsp.

⅛ cup = 1 oz.   = 2 tbs.
¼ cup = 2 oz.   = 4 tbs.
⅓ cup = 2⅔ oz.= 5⅓ tbs.
⅜ cup = 3 oz.   = ¼ cup plus 2 tbs.
½ cup = 4 oz.   = 8 tbs.

⅝ cup = 5 oz.   = ½ cup plus 2 tbs.
⅔ cup = 5⅓ oz.= 10⅔ tbs.
¾ cup = 6 oz.   = 12 tbs.
⅞ cup = 7 oz.   = ¾ cup plus 2 tbs.
1 cup = 8 oz.   = 16 tbs.

Tripling of ingredients

Use this chart for ingredients which may be tripled, such as when using fresh herbs instead of the dried herbs. If substituting fructose for a white or brown/maple sugar, use one third the amount, reading the table backwards.

¼ tsp. = ¾ tsp.
⅓ tsp. = 1 tsp.
½ tsp. = 1½ tsp.
¾ tsp. = 2¼ tsp.

⅔ tsp. = 2 tsp.
1 tsp. = 1 tbs.
1½ tsp. = 1½ tbs.
2 tsp. = 2 tbs.

Egg substitutions and equivalents

1 egg = ¼ cup dairy egg substitute
= ¼ cup additional liquid
= 1½ tsp. egg powder and 2 tbs. water

½ egg = 2 tbs. dairy egg substitute
= 2 tbs. additional liquid
= one egg white or one egg yolk
= ¾ tsp. egg powder and 1 tbs. water

WHITE AND CHEESE BREADS

WHITE POTATO BREAD

What a different and incredibly easy way to enjoy potato bread. The loaf is a low rising loaf which is easy to cut and is great for sandwiches or with a spicy stew. Potato should be uncooked, peeled and diced or grated.

	Small	Medium	Large
milk	2/3 cup	7/8 cup	1 cup
potato	1/4 cup	1/4+ cup	1/3 cup
vegetable oil	1 tsp.	1 1/4 tsp.	1 1/2 tsp.
sugar	1 tbs.	1 1/2 tbs.	2 tbs.
salt	1/3 tsp.	2/3 tsp.	1 tsp.
bread flour	2 cups	2 1/2 cups	3 cups
yeast	1 tsp.	1 1/2 tsp.	2 tsp.

flour equivalents:	*2 cups*	*2 1/2 cups*	*3 cups*
cycle:	*white; no timer (milk)*		
setting:	*light to medium*		

NO FAT WHITE BREAD

This is a light, easy-to-cut sandwich bread with a nice fluffy texture and a pleasant flavor.

	Small	**Medium**	**Large**
water	⅔ cup	¾ cup	1 cup
egg	1	1	1½
sugar	1 tsp.	1¼ tsp.	1½ tsp.
salt	⅛ tsp.	⅛+ tsp.	¼ tsp.
bread flour	2 cups	2½ cups	3 cups
yeast	1 tsp.	1½ tsp.	2 tsp.

flour equivalents:	*2 cups*	*2½ cups*	*3 cups*
cycle:	*white; no timer (egg)*		
setting:	*medium*		

NO SUGAR SWEET BREAD

For those who cannot or prefer not to eat refined sugar, this delicious recipe uses natural fructose which may be found in grocery stores or health food stores. One tester experimented with her recipe by substituting Sugar Twin for the fructose. She recommends using 1 tbs., 1½ tbs. or 2 tbs. for a regular loaf and doubling that amount for a sweeter loaf.

	Small	**Medium**	**Large**
milk	⅔ cup	¾ cup	1 cup
eggs	1	1½	2
margarine/butter	1 tbs.	1½ tbs.	2 tbs.
fructose	2 tsp.	1⅛ tbs.	1½ tbs.
salt	⅛ tsp.	⅛+ tsp.	¼ tsp.
bread flour	2 cups	2½ cups	3 cups
yeast	1 tsp.	1½ tsp.	2 tsp.
flour equivalents:	*2 cups*	*2½ cups*	*3 cups*
cycle:	*white, sweet; no timer (milk, egg)*		
setting:	*light to medium*		

FRUIT-FLAVORED BASIC WHITE BREAD

A delicious white bread using no refined sugar or fat. Select your favorite fruit juice concentrate to lightly flavor the bread. I use frozen juice concentrate (orange or apple) which has been thawed.

	Small	**Medium**	**Large**
milk/water	3/4 cup	1 cup	1 1/8 cups
fruit juice concentrate	2 tbs.	2 1/2 tbs.	3 tbs.
salt	1/4 tsp.	1/3 tsp.	1/2 tsp.
bread flour	2 cups	2 1/2 cups	3 cups
yeast	1 tsp.	1 1/2 tsp.	2 tsp.

flour equivalent:	*2 cups*	*2 1/2 cups*	*3 cups*
cycle:	*white, timer with water*		
setting:	*medium*		

COFFEE CAN BREAD

Karen Adler has made this bread for at least 20 years. She has adapted the recipe to her bread machine and no longer needs the coffee cans! She says it reminds her of challah, a Jewish egg bread. It is not one of the most dietetic. Karen has a DAK machine and makes the large loaf without suffering from the "doughy blues." If your machine is prone to doughiness, I recommend cutting the oil in half and replacing it with milk.

	Small	**Medium**	**Large**
milk	¼ cup	5 tbs.	⅜ cup
vegetable oil	¼ cup	5 tbs.	⅜ cup
eggs	1½	1½	2
sugar	2 tbs.	2½ tbs.	3 tbs.
salt	½ tsp.	⅔ tsp.	¾ tsp.
bread flour	2 cups	2½ cups	3 cups
yeast	1 tsp.	1½ tsp.	2 tsp.
flour equivalents:	*2 cups*	*2½ cups*	*3 cups*
cycle:	*white, sweet; no timer (milk, egg)*		
setting:	*light*		

CHEESE AND POPPY SEED BREAD

This is worth the extra calories as a special treat. Suggested cheeses are Swiss or cheddar. This dough will be stickier and moister than normal. It is a very high rising loaf. The cheese should be lightly packed in the measuring cup.

	Small	**Medium**	**Large**
milk	½ cup	5⁄8 cup	2⁄3 cup
eggs	2½	3	4
margarine/butter	5 tbs.	6½ tbs.	8 tbs.
lemon extract	2⁄3 tsp.	3⁄4 tsp.	1 tsp.
grated cheese	2⁄3 cup	3⁄4 cup	1 cup
sugar	1 tsp.	1½ tsp.	2 tsp.
lemon peel	2⁄3 tsp.	3⁄4 tsp.	1 tsp.
salt	½ tsp.	2⁄3 tsp.	1 tsp.
poppy seeds	1⅓ tbs.	1½ tbs.	2 tbs.
bread flour	2 cups	2½ cups	3 cups
yeast	1 tsp.	1½ tsp.	2 tsp.

flour equivalent: *2 cups*   *2½ cups*   *3 cups*
cycle: *white, sweet; no timer (milk, egg)*
setting: *medium*

BUTTERMILK CHEESE BREAD

An absolutely delicious, light and airy bread. I made the medium size recipe using a 2-cup machine and it hit the lid of the machine and mushroomed. It was still completely edible and delicious but the lid required cleaning! Cheddar is my favorite cheese to use in this.

	Small	Medium	Large
buttermilk	2/3 cup	3/4 cup	1 cup
margarine/butter	1 tbs.	1½ tbs.	2 tbs.
egg(s)	1	1½	2
grated cheese	½ cup	3/4 cup	1 cup
baking soda	¼ tsp.	1/3 tsp.	½ tsp.
sugar	1 tsp.	1½ tsp.	2 tsp.
salt	1/8 to ¼ tsp.	¼ to ½ tsp.	½ to 3/4 tsp.
bread flour	2 cups	2½ cups	3 cups
yeast	1 tsp.	1½ tsp.	2 tsp.

flour equivalent: *2 cups*   *2½ cups*   *3 cups*
cycle: *white, sweet; no timer (buttermilk, egg)*
setting: *light to medium*

CHEDDAR RAISIN BREAD

The testers give this one four stars! Absolutely delicious, a light texture with a pretty color and wonderful flavor! If the dough appears crumbly, feel free to add a tablespoon or so of milk, but don't add too much.

	Small	**Medium**	**Large**
milk	2/3 cup	3/4 cup	1 cup
margarine/butter	1 1/3 tbs.	1 1/2 tbs.	2 tbs.
grated cheddar	2/3 cup	3/4 cup	1 cup
paprika	2/3 tsp.	3/4 tsp.	1 tsp.
sugar	2 tsp.	1 tbs.	1 1/3 tbs.
salt	1/4 tsp.	1/3 tsp.	1/2 tsp.
bread flour	2 cups	2 1/2 cups	3 cups
yeast	1 tsp.	1 1/2 tsp.	2 tsp.
————			
raisins (dark)	1/3 cup	1/2 cup	2/3 cup

flour equivalents:	*2 cups*	*2 1/2 cups*	*3 cups*
cycle:	*raisin/mix; white, sweet*		
setting:	*medium*		

DATED PEASANT BREAD

The bread has just a hint of different flavor and has no fat or refined sugar. Due to the high liquid content, the texture is open and coarse. If desired, chopped dates may be added on the raisin/mix cycle, at the beeps (or when appropriate for your machine). Also, brown or granulated maple sugar could be used in place of the date sugar.

	Small	**Medium**	**Large**
water	1 cup	1¼ cups	1½ cups
date sugar	1 tsp.	1¼ tsp.	1½ tsp.
salt	⅛ tsp.	⅛+ tsp.	¼ tsp.
bread flour	2 cups	2½ cups	3 cups
yeast	1 tsp.	1½ tsp.	2 tsp.
chopped dates, optional	2 to 3 tbs.	3 tbs.	3 to 4 tbs.
flour equivalent:	*2 cups*	*2½ cups*	*3 cups*
cycle:	*white, timer*		
setting:	*medium*		

EASY CAKE BREAD

Rebecca O'Dea had her bread machine for only 10 days when she experimented with this recipe. She says it reminds her of the Hawaiian Bread from a local deli. The bread rises quite a bit during the baking program, and is very light and fluffy with a crisp crust. The variations to this are endless — try using different cake mixes such as devil's food, white or vanilla, etc. Orange or lemon peel (1/4-1 tsp.) could be added or even an extract (1/4-1/2 tsp.) for added flavor. This is an easy bread to make as all the sugar and salt are in the cake mix!

	Small	**Medium**	**Large**
water or milk	7/8 cup	1 cup	1 1/4 cups
butter/margarine	1 tbs.	1 1/2 tbs.	2 tbs.
yellow cake mix	2/3 cup	3/4 cup	1 cup
bread flour	1 1/4 cups	1 3/4 cups	2 1/2 cups
yeast	1 tsp.	1 1/2 tsp.	2 tsp.

flour equivalents:	*scant 2 cups*	*2 1/2 cups*	*3 1/2 cups*
cycle:	*white, sweet; timer with water*		
setting:	*light*		

HAITIAN BREAD

A beautiful, high rising, fluffy loaf which is sweet but not overly so. Nutmeg may be adjusted to taste, if desired. If you have never tried freshly grated nutmeg, I urge you to do so (even though my motto is "make it simple and easy"). Whole nutmegs are available in the spice section of a well stocked grocery. Simply grate it on a basic kitchen food grater. Try serving with ham and pineapple for a real treat! If desired, cinnamon may be substituted for the nutmeg.

	Small	Medium	Large
water	2/3 cup	3/4 cup	1 cup
vegetable oil	1 tbs.	1 1/3 tbs.	1 1/2 tbs.
honey	2 tbs.	2 1/2 tbs.	3 tbs.
salt	1/4 tsp.	1/4+ tsp.	1/3 tsp.
nutmeg	1/3 tsp.	1/3+ tsp.	1/2 tsp.
bread flour	2 cups	2 1/2 cups	3 cups
yeast	1 tsp.	1 1/2 tsp.	2 tsp.
flour equivalents:	*2 cups*	*2 1/2 cups*	*3 cups*
cycle:	*white, sweet; timer*		
setting:	*light to medium*		

BLUE CHEESE BREAD

A wonderful accompaniment to soup and salad. Should you have leftovers, try making croutons. A high rising, light loaf.

	Small	Medium	Large
water	2/3 cup	7/8 cup	1 cup
butter/margarine	1 tbs.	1¼ tbs.	1½ tbs.
blue cheese	1/3 cup	scant ½ cup	½ cup heaped
sugar	1 tbs.	1¼ tbs.	1½ tbs.
celery seeds	¼ tsp.	1/3 tsp.	scant ½ tsp.
salt	¼ to ½ tsp.	1/3 to 2/3 tsp.	½ to 1 tsp.
bread flour	2 cups	2½ cups	3 cups
yeast	1 tsp.	1½ tsp.	2 tsp.

flour equivalents:	*2 cups*	*2½ cups*	*3 cups*
cycle:	*white; no timer (cheese)*		
setting:	*medium*		

BROCCOLI AND CHEESE BREAD

Lots of nice, mild flavor with a wonderful aroma. Serve with pork chops or soup and salad. The broccoli should be cooked and chopped; the amount may be adjusted to taste if desired. Suggested cheeses are Swiss or cheddar; pack cheese lightly in the cup.

	Small	**Medium**	**Large**
milk	3/4 cup	1 1/8 cups	1 1/2 cups
margarine	1 tbs.	1 1/2 tbs.	2 tbs.
sugar	1 tsp.	1 1/2 tsp.	2 tsp.
salt	1/4 tsp.	1/3 tsp.	1/2 tsp.
whole wheat flour	1 cup	1 1/2 cups	2 cups
bread flour	1 cup	1 1/2 cups	2 cups
yeast	1 tsp.	1 1/2 tsp.	2 tsp.
broccoli	1/2 cup	3/4 cup	1 cup
cheese, grated	1/3 cup	1/2 cup	2/3 cup
flour equivalents:	*2 cups*	*3 cups*	*4 cups*
cycle:	*raisin/mix, white*		
setting:	*medium*		

WHOLE WHEAT, GRAIN AND CEREAL BREADS

BUTTERMILK HONEY WHEAT BREAD

Peg Timney of southern California shares her favorite recipe which she adapted for bread machine use.

	Small	Medium	Large
buttermilk	1 cup	1¼ cups	1½ cups
butter/margarine	1 tbs.	1⅓ tbs.	1½ tbs.
honey	2 tbs.	2½ tbs.	3 tbs.
salt	¾ tsp.	1 tsp.	1½ tsp.
baking soda	¼ tsp.	⅓ tsp.	½ tsp.
bread flour	1⅓ cups	1¾ cups	2 cups
whole wheat flour	⅔ cup	¾ cup	1 cup
yeast	1 tsp.	1½ tsp.	2 tsp.

flour equivalents:	*2 cups*	*2½ cups*	*3 cups*
cycle:	*white, sweet; no timer (buttermilk)*		
setting:	*light to medium*		

HONEY WHOLE WHEAT - NO FAT

This is in response to many requests for no fat or very low fat breads. The honey is a natural preservative as well as a sweetener. Great with chicken salad or toasted for breakfast.

	Small	Medium	Large
water	¾ cup	1⅛ cups	1½ cups
honey	2 tbs.	3 tbs.	¼ cup
salt	¼ tsp.	⅓ tsp.	½ tsp.
whole wheat flour	1 cup	1½ cups	2 cups
bread flour	1 cup	1½ cups	2 cups
yeast	1 tsp.	1½ tsp.	2 tsp.

flour equivalents:	*2 cups*	*3 cups*	*4 cups*
cycle:	*white; timer*		
setting:	*medium*		

CREAMY BUTTERMILK WHEAT BREAD

An outstanding bread. For variations, add 1, 1½ or 2 tablespoons of dried dill, chives, mint, basil or oregano (triple this amount for fresh).

	Small	**Medium**	**Large**
buttermilk	½ cup	¾ cup	1 cup
heavy cream	2½ tbs.	¼ cup	⅓ cup
butter	1 tbs.	1½ tbs.	2 tbs.
egg	1	1½	2
sugar	1 tbs.	1½ tbs.	2 tbs.
salt	⅛ to ¼ tsp.	¼ to ⅓ tsp.	⅓ to ½ tsp.
baking soda	¼ tsp.	⅓ tsp.	½ tsp.
bread flour	1 cup	1½ cups	2 cups
whole wheat flour	1 cup	1½ cups	2 cups
yeast	1 tsp.	1½ tsp.	2 tsp.

flour equivalents:	*2 cups*	*3 cups*	*4 cups*
cycle:	*white, sweet; no timer (buttermilk, cream, egg)*		
setting:	*light to medium*		

CARRIS' WHEAT BREAD

Carris House Jr. has been baking bread for years and now loves his bread machine for the ease and convenience it offers. Carris recommends using a blend of 50% Pillsbury bread flour and 50% Gold Medal bread flour. He also recommends using Stone Buhr stone ground wheat flour, if you can find it in your area!

	Small	**Medium**	**Large**
milk	1/4 cup	3/8 cup	1/2 cup
water	1/2 cup	3/4 cup	1 cup
margarine/butter	1 tbs.	1 1/2 tbs.	2 tbs.
molasses	2 tsp.	1 tbs.	1 1/3 tbs.
sugar	1 1/3 tbs.	2 tbs.	2 2/3 tbs.
salt	2/3 tsp.	1 tsp.	1 1/3 tsp.
bread flour	1 1/3 cups	2 cups	2 2/3 cups
whole wheat flour	2/3 cup	1 cup	1 1/3 cups
yeast	1 tsp.	1 1/2 tsp.	2 tsp.

flour equivalents:	*2 cups*	*3 cups*	*4 cups*
cycle:	*white, sweet; no timer (milk)*		
setting:	*light to medium*		

PORCUPINE BREAD

Don Downer adapted this recipe to his bread machine and receives rave reviews. Near the end of the second rising, Don lifts the lid and brushes the top of the loaf with an egg wash and sprinkles on additional sunflower and sesame seeds.

	Small	**Medium**	**Large**
buttermilk	3/4 cups	1 1/8 cups	1 1/2 cups
butter/margarine	1 tbs.	1 1/2 tbs.	2 tbs.
sugar	1 tbs.	1 1/2 tbs.	2 tbs.
salt	1/2 tsp.	3/4 tsp.	1 tsp.
baking soda	1/4 tsp.	1/3 tsp.	1/2 tsp.
cinnamon	1 tsp.	1 1/2 tsp.	2 tsp.
sesame seeds	1 tbs.	1 1/2 tbs.	2 tbs.
sunflower seeds	2 tbs.	3 tbs.	4 tbs.
raisins	1/4 cup	1/3 cup	1/2 cup
oats	1/4 cup	1/3 cup	1/2 cup
bread flour	1 3/4 cups	2 2/3 cups	3 1/2 cups
yeast	1 tsp.	1 1/2 tsp.	2 tsp.
flour equivalents:	*2 cups*	*3 cups*	*4 cups*
cycle:	*white; no timer (buttermilk)*		
setting:	*medium*		

IRISH BROWN BREAD

A crispy crust with a firm yet airy inside. Rises nicely.

	Small	**Medium**	**Large**
water	¾ cup	1⅛ cups	1½ cups
brown sugar	2 tbs.	3 tbs.	¼ cup
salt	⅓ tsp.	½ tsp.	⅔ tsp.
bread flour	1 cup	1½ cups	2 cups
vital gluten, optional	2 tbs.	3 tbs.	¼ cup
oats	⅓ cup	½ cup	⅔ cup
wheat flour	¾ cup	1 cup	1½ cups
buttermilk powder	2 tbs.	3 tbs.	¼ cup
yeast	1½ tsp.	2 tsp.	2½ tsp.

flour equivalents:	*2+ cups*	*3 cups*	*4+ cups*
cycle:	*whole grain, white; timer*		
setting:	*medium*		

OATMEAL HONEY RAISIN BREAD

Patricia Harper of Louisiana dreamed this one up. She actually uses more raisins, but I cut them back as some machines have more difficulty cooking properly with too many raisins or similar ingredients. If desired, use fresh buttermilk in place of the water, omit the powder and add 1/8 to 1/4 tsp. of baking soda. This bread is also delicious without the raisins!

	Small	**Medium**	**Large**
water	7/8 cup	1 1/4 cups	1 3/4 cups
vegetable oil	1 tbs.	1 1/2 tbs.	2 tbs.
honey	1 1/3 tbs.	2 tbs.	2 1/2 tbs.
salt	1/2 tsp.	3/4 tsp.	1 tsp.
bread flour	1 1/3 cups	2 cups	2 2/3 cups
oats (quick/reg)	2/3 cup	1 cup	1 1/3 cups
buttermilk powder	1 1/3 tbs.	2 tbs.	2 1/2 tbs.
yeast	1 tsp.	1 1/2 tsp.	2 tsp.
———			
raisins	1/2 cup	3/4 cup	1 cup
flour equivalents:	*2 cups*	*3 cups*	*4 cups*
cycle:	*raisin/mix; white, sweet*		
setting:	*light to medium*		

HEALTHY WHOLE WHEAT BREAD

This is an especially healthy, sweet whole wheat bread from Conrad Feierabend.

	Small	Medium	Large
water	5⁄8 cup	1 cup	1¼ cups
vegetable oil	1⅓ tbs.	2 tbs.	2½ tbs.
molasses	1½ tbs.	2⅓ tbs.	3 tbs.
salt	½ tsp.	¾ tsp.	1 tsp.
fructose	2 tsp.	1 tbs.	1½ tbs.
sesame seeds	½ tsp.	¾ tsp.	1 tsp.
oat groats, cracked	1½ tsp.	2 tsp.	1 tbs.
wheat germ	2 tsp.	1 tbs.	1⅓ tbs.
oat bran	2 tsp.	1 tbs.	1⅓ tbs.
wheat flakes	2 tsp.	1 tbs.	1⅓ tbs.
oats	1 tbs.	1½ tbs.	2 tbs.
wheat flour	½ cup	¾ cup	1 cup
bread flour	1 cup	1½ cups	2 cups
yeast	1½ tsp.	2 tsp.	2½ tsp.
flour equivalents:	*scant 2 cups*	*2⅔ cups*	*3½ cups*
cycle:	*white, sweet; timer*		
setting:	*medium*		

BIMINI BREAD

Gerry Milot has been served this bread at the Bimini Boat Yard, a restaurant in Ft. Lauderdale. He modified the recipe for the bread machines. Gerry soaks the oats, molasses and butter in hot water for 2 minutes and then adds them to the bread machine. I put everything in all at once, unsoaked. A nice, wholesome bread.

	Small	**Medium**	**Large**
water	¾ cup	1⅛ cups	1½ cups
vegetable oil	1 tbs.	1½ tbs.	2 tbs.
molasses	1½ tbs.	1⅓ tbs.	3 tbs.
salt	⅓ tsp.	½ tsp.	⅔ tsp.
bread flour	1½ cups	2¼ cups	3 cups
oats	½ cup	¾ cup	1 cup
yeast	1 tsp.	1½ tsp.	2 tsp.

flour equivalents:	*2 cups*	*3 cups*	*4 cups*
cycle:	*white, sweet; timer*		
setting:	*light to medium*		

ANADAMA BREAD

Anadama is one of those breads which has several different variations. The commonality is that each recipe uses molasses and cornmeal. Katherine Kuckens adapted her mother's recipe for use in her bread machine. A hearty bread to serve with soup and salad!

	Small	Medium	Large
water	1 cup	1¼ cups	1½ cups
oil or butter	1½ tsp.	2 tsp.	2¼ tsp.
molasses	¼ cup	5 tbs.	6 tbs.
salt	½ tsp.	⅔ tsp.	¾ tsp.
cornmeal	¼ cup	⅓ cup	⅜ cup
bread flour	2 cups	2½ cups	3 cups
yeast	1½ tsp.	2 tsp.	2½ tsp.

flour equivalents:	*2¼ cups*	*2¾+ cups*	*3⅜ cups*
cycle:	*white, sweet; timer*		
setting:	*light to medium*		

COCONUT CORN BREAD

Based on a recipe from the Dominican Republic. Soak the raisins in the rum for at least 30 minutes before putting into the machine at the normal time.

	Small	**Medium**	**Large**
milk/water	¾ cup	1⅛ cups	1½ cups
butter/margarine	1 tbs.	1½ tbs.	2 tbs.
sugar	2 tbs.	3 tbs.	¼ cup
salt	½ tsp.	¾ tsp.	1 tsp.
cinnamon	½ tsp.	¾ tsp.	1 tsp.
ground cloves	¼ tsp.	⅓ tsp.	½ tsp.
shredded coconut	½ cup	¾ cup	1 cup
cornmeal	½ cup	¾ cup	1 cup
bread flour	1½ cups	2¼ cups	3 cups
yeast	1 tsp.	1½ tsp.	2 tsp.
─────			
rum	1 tbs.	1½ tbs.	2 tbs.
raisins	¼ cup	⅓ cup	½ cup
flour equivalents:	*2 cups*	*3 cups*	*4 cups*
cycle:	*raisin/mix; white, sweet*		
setting:	*light*		

CORNMEAL ENGLISH MUFFIN BREAD

Dee Iuliano of New Mexico makes this cornmeal in her bread machine. She says it's similar to the English muffin bread; hence, the name. For variety, try using blue cornmeal!

	Small	**Medium**	**Large**
water	¾ cup	1⅛ cups	1½ cups
egg	½	1 small	1 large
sugar	2 tsp.	1 tbs.	1⅓ tbs.
salt	½ tsp.	¾ tsp.	1 tsp.
cornmeal	½ cup	¾ cup	1 cup
bread flour	1½ cups	2¼ cups	3 cups
yeast	1½ tsp.	2 tsp.	2½ tsp.

flour equivalents: *2 cups*   *3 cups*   *4 cups*
cycle: *white; no timer (egg)*
setting: *medium*

JALAPEÑO CORN BREAD

An outstanding bread for jalapeño lovers. Use either cheddar or Monterey Jack cheese. The jalapeños may be adjusted to taste; the amount of buttermilk may require some adjusting to compensate for more or less liquid from the peppers. Green chiles may be substituted if desired. I use either drained corn or frozen kernels which have been thawed. If fresh corn is available, that would be even better!

	Small	**Medium**	**Large**
buttermilk	¾ cup	1⅛ cups	1½ cups
corn kernels	⅓ cup	½ cup	⅔ cup
grated cheese	¼ cup	⅓ cup	½ cup
diced jalapeños	1	1½	2
honey	½ tsp.	¾ tsp.	1 tsp.
salt	¼ tsp.	⅓ tsp.	½ tsp.
baking soda	¼ tsp.	⅓ tsp.	½ tsp.
cornmeal	½ cup	¾ cup	1 cup
bread flour	1½ cups	2¼ cups	3 cups
yeast	1½ tsp.	2 tsp.	2½ tsp.
flour equivalents:	*2 cups*	*3 cups*	*4 cups*
cycle:	*white; timer*		
setting:	*medium*		

THREE SEED BARLEY RYE

A distinctive taste due to the seed and barley combination which is great with cream cheese — sprinkle some seeds on top of cheese for added flavor if desired. Since the high percentage of rye flour causes this to be a low-rising loaf, adding the vital gluten will help. Molasses or honey may be substituted for the barley malt.

	Small	**Medium**	**Large**
water	⅔ cup	1 cup	1⅓ cups
vegetable oil	1½ tbs.	2¼ tbs.	3 tbs.
barley malt syrup	1½ tbs.	2¼ tbs.	3 tbs.
salt	⅛ to ¼ tsp.	¼ to ⅓ tsp.	⅓ to ½ tsp.
anise seeds	½ tsp.	¾ tsp.	1 tsp.
fennel seeds	½ tsp.	¾ tsp.	1 tsp.
caraway seeds	½ tsp.	¾ tsp.	1 tsp.
rye flour	1 cup	1½ cups	2 cups
bread flour	1 cup	1½ cups	2 cups
vital gluten, optional	1 to 2 tbs.	1½ to 3 tbs.	2 to 4 tbs.
yeast	1½ tsp.	2 tsp.	2½ tsp.
flour equivalents:	*2 cups*	*3 cups*	*4 cups*
cycle:	*whole grain, white, sweet; timer*		
setting:	*medium*		

ORANGE POTATO RYE

What a combination — a potato bread with rye for a superb treat! Try substituting other seeds such as anise or fennel for a flavorful change of pace. Instead of mashing a potato, use a 4, 6 or 8 oz. cooked potato and let the machine mash it for you.

	Small	**Medium**	**Large**
mashed potato	½ cup	¾ cup	1 cup
potato water	⅓ cup	½ cup	⅔ cup
vegetable oil	1 tbs.	1½ tbs.	2 tbs.
honey/molasses	1 tbs.	1½ tbs.	2 tbs.
orange peel	¼ tsp.	⅓ tsp.	½ tsp.
salt	⅓ tsp.	½ tsp.	⅔ tsp.
caraway seeds, optional	1 tsp.	1½ tsp.	2 tsp.
rye flour	½ cup	¾ cup	1 cup
whole wheat flour	½ cup	¾ cup	1 cup
bread flour	1 cup	1½ cups	2 cups
yeast	1 tsp.	1½ tsp.	2 tsp.

flour equivalents:	*2 cups*	*3 cups*	*4 cups*
cycle:	*whole grain, white, sweet; timer (hour or so)*		
setting:	*medium*		

RYE AND CRACKED WHEAT BREAD

A low dense loaf without the gluten. If desired, add anise, fennel or caraway seeds for extra flavor (1/2 to 2 tsp. depending on taste). The cracked wheat must sit in the water for at least one hour. With the exception of the DAK, Welbilt and National/Panasonic machines, the cracked wheat may be soaked right in the pan if using the timer.

	Small	**Medium**	**Large**
water	3/4 cup	1 1/8 cups	1 1/2 cups
cracked wheat	1/2 cup	3/4 cup	1 cup
vegetable oil	1 tbs.	1 1/2 tbs.	2 tbs.
honey	2 tsp.	1 tbs.	1 1/3 tbs.
salt	1/8 tsp.	1/8+ tsp.	1/4 tsp.
bread flour	1 cup	1 1/2 cups	2 cups
rye flour	1/2 cup	3/4 cup	1 cup
vital gluten, optional	1 to 2 tbs.	1 1/2 to 3 tbs.	2 to 4 tbs.
yeast	1 1/2 tsp.	2 tsp.	2 1/2 tsp.
flour equivalents:	*2 cups*	*3 cups*	*4 cups*
cycle:	*whole grain, white, sweet; timer*		
setting:	*medium*		

RYE BERRY BREAD

This densely textured bread makes great sandwiches or toast. Watch the dough and add a tablespoon or two more of milk if needed to form a well rounded ball.

	Small	**Medium**	**Large**
water	1 cup	1½ cups	2 cups
rye berries	⅓ cup	½ cup	⅔ cups

Bring berries and water to a boil for approximately 5 minutes. Cover, remove from heat and allow to stand for about 6 to 8 hours or overnight. Drain berries prior to using.

milk	½ cup	¾ cup	1 cup
vegetable oil	1 tbs.	1½ tbs.	2 tbs.
honey	1 tbs.	1½ tbs.	2 tbs.
salt	⅟₁₆ tsp.	⅛ tsp.	⅛+ tsp.
caraway	1 tsp.	1½ tsp.	2 tsp.
vital gluten, optional	1 tbs.	1½ tbs.	2 tbs.
whole wheat flour	⅓ cup	½ cup	⅔ cup
rye flour	⅓ cup	½ cup	⅔ cup
bread flour	1 cup	1½ cups	2 cups
yeast	1½ tsp.	2 tsp.	2½ tsp.
flour equivalents:	*2 cups*	*3 cups*	*4 cups*
cycle:	*whole grain, white, sweet; timer*		
setting:	*medium*		

RYE HERB BREAD

A spicy, flavorful bread. The pepper, rosemary and parsley amounts may be adjusted to taste if desired. If using fresh herbs, triple the amount given. I use coarsely ground black pepper. A light, high-rising rye if using vital gluten.

	Small	**Medium**	**Large**
water	¾ cup	1⅛ cups	1½ cups
butter/margarine	2 tbs.	3 tbs.	4 tbs.
brown sugar	1 tbs.	1½ tbs.	2 tbs.
salt	¼ tsp.	⅓ tsp.	½ tsp.
black pepper	½ tsp.	¾ tsp.	1 tsp.
rosemary	½ tsp.	¾ tsp.	1 tsp.
parsley (dried)	1 tsp.	1½ tsp.	2 tsp.
whole wheat flour	⅔ cup	1 cup	1⅓ cups
rye flour	⅔ cup	1 cup	1⅓ cups
vital gluten, optional	1 to 2 tbs.	1½ to 3 tbs.	2 to 4 tbs.
bread flour	⅔ cup	1 cup	1⅓ cups
yeast	1½ tsp.	2 tsp.	2½ tsp.
flour equivalents:	*2 cups*	*3 cups*	*4 cups*
cycle:	*whole grain, white, sweet; timer*		
setting:	*light to medium*		

BEAN FLAKE RYE BREAD

This is an absolutely superb loaf of bread. A moist, tasty treat. Black bean flakes may be found in health food and some grocery stores. I use just the flakes but have seen black bean flake soup/dip mixes available. If using a mix, check the amount of salt and adjust (down) or even delete the salt from this recipe, if necessary.

	Small	Medium	Large
water/milk	¾ cup	1⅛ cups	1½ cups
vegetable oil	1 tbs.	1½ tbs.	2 tbs.
molasses	2 tbs.	3 tbs.	¼ cup
salt	¼ tsp.	⅓ tsp.	½ tsp.
black bean flakes	¼ cup	⅓ cup	½ cup
caraway seeds	1 tsp.	1½ tsp.	2 tsp.
orange peel, optional	¼ tsp.	⅓ tsp.	½ tsp.
rye flour	¾ cup	1 cup	1½ cups
vital gluten, optional	1 to 2 tbs.	1½ to 3 tbs.	2 to 4 tbs.
bread flour	1¼ cups	2 cups	2½ cups
yeast	1 tsp.	1½ tsp.	2 tsp.
flour equivalents:	*2 cups*	*3 cups*	*4 cups*
cycle:	*whole grain, white, sweet; timer with water*		
setting:	*medium*		

BEAN FLAKE PUMPERNICKEL

Black bean flakes provide this bread with some of its coloring as well as a distinctive taste and, of course, lots of added nutrients. Barley malt may be substituted for the molasses if desired. This is one of my favorites.

	Small	Medium	Large
water/milk	¾ cup	1⅛ cups	1½ cups
vegetable oil	1 tbs.	1½ tbs.	2 tbs.
molasses	2 tbs.	3 tbs.	¼ cup
salt	¼ tsp.	⅓ tsp.	½ tsp.
black bean flakes	¼ cup	⅓ cup	½ cup
instant coffee granules	1 tbs.	1½ tbs.	2 tbs.
unsweetened cocoa	1 tbs.	1½ tbs.	2 tbs.
caraway seeds	1 tsp.	1½ tsp.	2 tsp.
rye flour	½ cup	¾ cup	1 cup
whole wheat flour	½ cup	¾ cup	1 cup
bread flour	1 cup	1½ cups	2 cups
yeast	1 tsp.	1½ tsp.	2 tsp.

flour equivalents: *2 cups*   *3 cups*   *4 cups*
cycle: *whole grain, white, sweet; timer with water*
setting: *medium*

MUSTARD RYE

Kit Bie says to make sure to use a Dijon with the mustard seed grains as it gives the bread a nicer texture. Mustard seeds may be added if desired. A very moist bread which rises nicely and has a great taste as well as aroma! A "must try."

	Small	**Medium**	**Large**
water	2/3 cup	1 cup	1 1/3 cups
vegetable oil	2 tsp.	1 tbs.	1 1/3 tbs.
honey	1 tbs.	1 1/2 tbs.	2 tbs.
Dijon mustard	2 tbs.	3 tbs.	1/4 cup
salt	1/3 tsp.	1/2 tsp.	2/3 tsp.
mustard seeds, optional	1/2 tsp.	3/4 tsp.	1 tsp.
caraway/fennel, optional	1 tsp.	1 1/2 tsp.	2 tsp.
rye flour	2/3 cup	1 cup	1 1/3 cups
whole wheat flour	1/3 cup	1/2 cup	2/3 cup
bread flour	1 cup	1 1/2 cups	2 cups
vital gluten, optional	1 to 2 tbs.	1 1/2 to 3 tbs.	2 to 4 tbs.
yeast	1 1/2 tsp.	2 tsp.	2 1/2 tsp.
flour equivalents:	*2 cups*	*3 cups*	*4 cups*
cycle:	*whole grain, white, sweet; timer*		
setting:	*medium*		

JEWISH RYE CORNMEAL BREAD

A very small amount of gluten in both the rye and cornmeal results in this being a low-rising loaf of bread. I recommend using the vital gluten in this recipe. The combination of rye and cornmeal along with the wheat flour makes for a very nutritious loaf of bread.

	Small	**Medium**	**Large**
water	¾ cup	1⅛ cups	1½ cups
vegetable oil	1 tbs.	1½ tbs.	2 tbs.
honey	2 tbs.	2⅓ tbs.	3 tbs.
salt	¼ tsp.	⅓ tsp.	½ tsp.
caraway, optional	1 tsp.	1½ tsp.	2 tsp.
cornmeal	¼ cup	⅓ cup	½ cup
rye flour	½ cup	⅔ cup	1 cup
bread flour	1¼ cups	2 cups	2½ cups
vital gluten, optional	1 to 2 tbs.	1½ to 3 tbs.	2 to 4 tbs.
yeast	1½ tsp.	2 tsp.	2½ tsp.

flour equivalents:	*2 cups*	*3 cups*	*4 cups*
cycle:	*whole grain, white, sweet; timer*		
setting:	*medium*		

SLIGHTLY RYE BREAD

If using the caraway, it may be adjusted to your taste. Other seeds such as anise, fennel or sesame may be substituted. A low-rising, densely textured loaf with the distinct flavor of the seed and a slight rye taste. Wheat flakes are rolled, just like the oats, and may be found in health food stores.

	Small	Medium	Large
milk/water	¾ cup	1⅛ cups	1½ cups
vegetable oil	1½ tbs.	2¼ tbs.	3 tbs.
honey/molasses	2 tbs.	3 tbs.	¼ cup
salt	⅓ tsp.	½ tsp.	⅔ tsp.
caraway, optional	1½ tsp.	2 tsp.	1 tbs.
orange peel	¼ tsp.	⅓ tsp.	½ tsp.
vital gluten, optional	1 to 2 tbs.	1½ to 3 tbs.	2 to 4 tbs.
oat/wheat flakes	¾ cup	1⅛ cups	1½ cups
rye flour	¼ cup	⅓ cup	½ cup
bread flour	1 cup	1½ cups	2 cups
yeast	1 tsp.	1½ tsp.	2 tsp.
flour equivalents:	*2 cups*	*3 cups*	*4 cups*
cycle:	*whole grain, white, sweet; timer with water*		
setting:	*medium*		

DATED RYE

Date sugar (available in health food stores) replaces any refined sugar in this great sandwich bread.

	Small	Medium	Large
water	¾ cup	1⅛ cups	1½ cups
egg	1	1½	2
vegetable oil	1 tbs.	1½ tbs.	2 tbs.
date sugar	1 tsp.	1½ tsp.	2 tsp.
salt	⅛ to ¼ tsp.	¼ to ⅓ tsp.	⅓ to ½ tsp.
caraway seed	1½ tsp.	2¼ tsp.	3 tsp.
rye flour	1 cup	1½ cups	2 cups
vital gluten	1 to 2 tbs.	1½ to 3 tbs.	2 to 4 tbs.
bread flour	1 cup	1½ cups	2 cups
yeast	1½ tsp.	2 tsp.	2½ tsp.

flour equivalents: *2 cups*   *3 cups*   *4 cups*
cycle: *whole grain, white; no timer (egg)*
setting: *medium*

STOUT BREAD

This recipe was developed by Paul Dudley of Pillsford, NY. He uses "chocolate" malted barley which he purchases from a beer making supply company. Or use barley malt syrup, available from any health food store. Paul says that this bread is a wonderful accompaniment to any sandwich. The bread rises nicely.

	Small	**Medium**	**Large**
water	¾ cup	1 cup	1½ cups
vegetable oil	2 tsp.	1 tbs.	1½ tbs.
barley malt syrup	2 tsp.	1 tbs.	1½ tbs.
sugar (white/brown)	2 tsp.	1 tbs.	1½ tbs.
salt	⅓ tsp.	½ tsp.	¾ tsp.
bread flour	1⅓ cups	1¾ cups	2⅔ cups
whole wheat flour	1½ tbs.	2⅓ tbs.	3 tbs.
rye flour	1½ tbs.	2⅓ tbs.	3 tbs.
oats	1½ tbs.	2⅓ tbs.	3 tbs.
Roman meal	1½ tbs.	2⅓ tbs.	3 tbs.
yeast	1½ tsp.	2 tsp.	2½ tsp.
flour equivalents:	*1⅔ cups*	*2¼ cups*	*3⅜ cups*
cycle:	*whole grain, white, sweet; timer*		
setting:	*medium*		

RYE FLAKE BREAD

Janice Buttress adapted her mother's recipe to her bread machine. She suggests using the variations as well. Janice uses rapid rise yeast and bakes it right away. This is a very high rising, chewy bread. Rye flakes are similar to oat flakes (such as Quaker Oats) and may be found in health food stores.

	Small	**Medium**	**Large**
water	3/4 cup	1 1/8 cups	1 1/2 cups
vegetable oil	1 tsp.	1 1/2 tsp.	2 tsp.
honey	1 tsp.	1 1/2 tsp.	2 tsp.
salt	1/3 tsp.	1/2 tsp.	2/3 tsp.
bread flour	1 3/4 cups	2 2/3 cup	3 1/2 cups
rye flakes	1/4 cup	1/3 cup	1/2 cup
yeast	1 tsp.	1 1/2 tsp.	2 tsp.

Variations: add 1 of the following, or 2 if you cut the amounts in half:

cracked wheat	2 tbs.	3 tbs.	1/4 cup
9-grain cereal	2 tbs.	3 tbs.	1/4 cup
wheat germ	1 1/4 tbs.	2 tbs.	2 1/2 tbs.
flour equivalents:	*2 cups*	*3 cups*	*4 cups*
cycle:	*white; timer*		
setting:	*medium*		

WHEAT SOY SESAME BREAD

Janice Quinn made this bread before she discovered the wonders of bread machines. Adapted to fit the machines, this is still her favorite. Janice says to grind the sesame seeds in a blender before adding but I just add as usual. Janice uses soy grits but corn grits are more easily found and may be substituted. A low-rising loaf with lots of taste and an easy-to-cut texture.

	Small	Medium	Large
water	2/3 cup	1 cup	1 1/3 cups
vegetable oil	1 1/3 tbs.	2 tbs.	2 2/3 tbs.
honey	1 1/3 tbs.	2 tbs.	2 2/3 tbs.
sesame seeds	1/4 cup	1/3 cup	1/2 cup
soy powder or flour	2 2/3 tbs.	1/4 cup	5 1/3 tbs.
grits	2 tsp.	1 tbs.	1 1/3 tbs.
whole wheat flour	2/3 cup	1 cup	1 1/3 cups
bread flour	7/8 cup	1 1/4 cups	1 3/4 cups
yeast	1 tsp.	1 1/2 tsp.	2 tsp.

flour equivalents:	*scant 2 cups*	*scant 3 cups*	*scant 4 cups*
cycle:	*whole grain, white, sweet; timer*		
setting:	*light to medium*		

WHOLE WHEAT PEASANT BREAD

A nice flavor with a hint of something different. A basic no fat, no refined sugar bread. Either brown or maple sugar may be substituted for the date sugar.

	Small	Medium	Large
water	1 cup	1½ cups	2 cups
date sugar	1 tsp.	1½ tsp.	2 tsp.
salt	¼ tsp.	⅓ tsp.	½ tsp.
bread flour	1 cup	1½ cups	2 cups
whole wheat flour	1 cup	1½ cups	2 cups
yeast	1 tsp.	1½ tsp.	2 tsp.

flour equivalents:	2 cups	3 cups	4 cups
cycle:	white; timer		
setting:	medium		

MAPLE BRAN BREAD

The maple syrup imparts a delicate, sweet taste while the bran adds to the nutritional value of this great loaf of bread.

	Small	**Medium**	**Large**
milk	¾ cup	1⅛ cups	1½ cups
vegetable oil	1 tbs.	1½ tbs.	2 tbs.
maple syrup	2 tbs.	3 tbs.	¼ cup
salt	¼ tsp.	⅓ tsp.	½ tsp.
oat/wheat bran	¼ cup	⅓ cup	½ cup
whole wheat flour	½ cup	¾ cup	1 cup
bread flour	1½ cups	2¼ cups	3 cups
yeast	1½ tsp.	2 tsp.	2½ tsp.
———			
raisins, optional	¼ cup	⅓ cup	½ cup

flour equivalents:	*2 cups*	*3 cups*	*4 cups*
cycle:	*raisin/mix; white, sweet*		
setting:	*medium*		

SOURDOUGHS

Sourdough recipes have been among the most requested. One thing that I keep hearing, however, is that people want it to be easy — making and caring for the starter initially seems intimidating. The solution is very simple as starters may be purchased easily. For testing purposes, I used two different starters. Baker's Catalog from King Arthur Flour sells a starter which is in a liquid form. It is a compilation of several different starters, including one each from San Francisco, Alaska and the New England area. Ordered through their mail order catalog, they cannot ship during the hot summer months. The other starter I used is more readily available in grocery and gourmet stores as well as by mail order. Called Goldrush Sourdough Starter, this is a dried starter which is purchased in small packets. The contents of both starters are mixed with just flour and water (fed) and are ready for use within a day or so; follow the directions with your purchased starter. I was very pleased with both. Each starter had a different thickness which may be adjusted by simply adding more or less liquid during feedings. Over most of the testing period the starters were used individually but towards the end they were combined for a new taste.

To make your own starter, mix together in a glass or plastic bowl:

2 cups lukewarm (baby bottle) water or milk
2 cups bread or unbleached all purpose flour
2½ tsp. (1 pkg.) yeast

Cover the bowl and allow to sit in a warm, draft-free location for 4 to 7 days, gently stirring once a day. You may notice that the mixture bubbles and may even overflow the bowl; this is an indication of the fermentation going on. It is also common for the starter to bubble up and then collapse if moved or jarred somehow. A sour smelling liquid may form on top of the starter which may simply be stirred back into the starter prior to use. It is generally recommended that you stir your starter with a wooden or plastic spoon.

To use your starter, simply remove the amount called for in the recipe and add to the other ingredients. Replace the amount removed with equal amounts of water/milk and bread/unbleached all purpose flour. I always use bread flour. For example, if one cup of starter is used in your recipe, stir one cup of water and one cup of flour back into the mixture; this is called "feeding" your starter.

Allow the starter to sit in a warm, draft-free location for approximately 24 hours after which time it may be used again or refrigerated.

A starter must be used at least once a week; or remove a portion (usually one cup) and throw that away. Feed as usual. If this is not done, your starter will become rancid as it requires fresh flour to feed on. Should you be away from your starter, freeze it and then thaw it in the refrigerator upon your return. As soon as it is thawed, it may be fed as above.

The longer the starter is used, the stronger it becomes in flavor. For many people developing and using their own starter is part of the fun and excitement; for other people, it seems easier and more fun to purchase one which already has lots of flavor and strength and has a "story" behind it.

IMPORTANT! Sourdough starters develop their own personalities and flavors; some may be thicker than others depending on variables such as the type of flour and liquid used. For this reason it is imperative to watch the dough as it kneads. I recommend that you allow the machine to knead the dough for approximately 3-5 minutes and then check it to see if it has formed a nice round dough ball. If not, add a tablespoon of water or flour at a time until it does so.

You may even want to keep notes if necessary. Once you have a good "feel" for the need to add more water or flour than the recipes call for, you could begin to use the timer cycle with your changes already made.

SOURDOUGH ONION RYE

This is out of this world. Try using anise instead of caraway for a wonderful twist on an old favorite. As with any rye bread, this tends to be a low-rising loaf.

	Small	Medium	Large
starter	½ cup	¾ cup	1 cup
water/milk	⅓ cup	½ cup	⅔ cup
diced onion	¼ cup	⅓ cup	½ cup
vegetable oil	1 tbs.	1½ tbs.	2 tbs.
molasses	2 tbs.	3 tbs.	¼ cup
salt	½ tsp.	¾ tsp.	1 tsp.
caraway seeds, optional	2 tsp.	1 tbs.	1⅓ tbs.
vital gluten	1 to 2 tbs.	1½ to 3 tbs.	2 to 4 tbs.
rye flour	½ cup	¾ cup	1 cup
bread flour	1½ cups	2¼ cups	3 cups
yeast	1 tsp.	1½ tsp.	2 tsp.

flour equivalents:	*2¼ cups*	*3⅓ cups*	*4½ cups*
cycle:	*whole grain, sweet, white; timer with water*		
setting:	*medium*		

SOURDOUGH PUMPERNICKEL

Outstanding! The cocoa and instant coffee granules provide color for this bread; black bean flour could be substituted for the cocoa if available. (I grind my own in an electric flour mill). Caraway may be adjusted to taste.

	Small	Medium	Large
starter	½ cup	¾ cup	1 cup
water	½ cup	¾ cup	1 cup
vegetable oil	1 tbs.	1½ tbs.	2 tbs.
molasses	2 tbs.	3 tbs.	¼ cup
unsweetened cocoa	1 tbs.	1½ tbs.	2 tbs.
instant coffee granules	1 tsp.	1½ tsp.	2 tsp.
salt	½ tsp.	¾ tsp.	1 tsp.
caraway seeds, optional	2 tsp.	1 tbs.	1⅓ tbs.
rye flour	½ cup	¾ cup	1 cup
whole wheat flour	½ cup	¾ cup	1 cup
bread flour	1 cup	1½ cups	2 cups
yeast	1½ tsp.	2 tsp.	2½ tsp.
flour equivalents:	*2½ cups*	*3⅓ cups*	*4½ cups*
cycle:	*whole grain, white, sweet; timer*		
setting:	*medium*		

SOURDOUGH PEASANT BREAD

Art Cazares took two of his favorite breads and combined them to come up with this one. Art uses much more water than I have listed. Feel free to increase the water if desired.

	Small	Medium	Large
sourdough starter	¾ cup	1⅛ cups	1½ cups
water	⅓ cup	½ cup	⅔ cup
sugar	1 tsp.	1¼ tsp.	1½ tsp.
salt	½ tsp.	¾ tsp.	1 tsp.
bread flour	1½ cups	2¼ cups	3 cups
yeast	1 tsp.	1½ tsp.	2 tsp.

flour equivalents:	1⅞ cups	2¾ cups	3¾ cups
cycle:	whole grain, white, sweet; timer		
setting:	medium		

SOURDOUGH FRENCH BREAD

This delicious, pungent sour French bread goes nicely with cheese and wine.

	Small	**Medium**	**Large**
starter	½ cup	¾ cup	1 cup
water	½ cup	¾ cup	1 cup
salt	½ tsp.	¾ tsp.	1 tsp.
sugar	⅓ tsp.	½ tsp.	⅔ tsp.
wheat flour	1 cup	1½ cups	2 cups
all purpose flour	1 cup	1½ cups	2 cups
yeast	1 tsp.	1½ tsp.	2 tsp.
cornmeal for shaping			

Allow the dough to rise in the machine for at least 1½ hours — even if the machine has stopped. Punch down the dough while it is still in the pan in the machine and allow it to rise in the turned off but still warm machine or other warm, draft-free location for 30 to 40 minutes. See page 147 for shaping and baking guidelines.

flour equivalents:	*2¼ cups*	*3⅓ cups*	*4½ cups*
cycle:	*dough*		

SOURDOUGH MAPLE WALNUT BREAD

A twist on a basic sourdough which is good even without the nuts!

	Small	Medium	Large
starter	½ cup	¾ cup	1 cup
milk or water	½ cup	¾ cup	1 cup
walnut oil	1 tbs.	1½ tbs.	2 tbs.
maple syrup	2 tbs.	3 tbs.	¼ cup
cinnamon, optional	¼ tsp.	⅓ tsp.	½ tsp.
salt	⅓ tsp.	½ tsp.	⅔ tsp.
whole wheat flour	1 cup	1½ cups	2 cups
bread flour	1 cup	1½ cups	2 cups
yeast	1 tsp.	1½ tsp.	2 tsp.
——			
chopped walnuts	¼ cup	⅓ cup	½ cup
raisins, optional	¼ cup	⅓ cup	½ cup
flour equivalents:	*2¼ cups*	*3⅓ cups*	*4½ cups*
cycle:	*raisin/mix; whole grain, sweet, white*		
setting:	*light to medium*		

QUICK SOUR PUMPERNICKEL

You'll enjoy this easy sourdough.

starter	Small	Medium	Large
milk	3/4 cup	1 1/8 cups	1 1/2 cups
rye flour	1 cup	1 1/2 cups	2 cups
gluten	1 tbs.	1 1/2 tbs.	2 tbs.
yeast	1 tsp.	1 1/2 tsp.	2 tsp.

Let starter ingredients knead for about 10 minutes and then sit in the pan in the machine overnight or for 6 to 8 hours. Add remaining ingredients and start machine as usual.

coffee	1/4 cup	1/3 cup	1/2 cup
vegetable oil	1 tbs.	1 1/2 tbs.	2 tbs.
molasses	2 tbs.	3 tbs.	1/4 cup
unsweetened cocoa	1 tbs.	1 1/2 tbs.	2 tbs.
salt	1/4 tsp.	1/3 tsp.	1/2 tsp.
caraway/fennel	1 tsp.	1 1/2 tsp.	2 tsp.
whole wheat flour	1/2 cup	3/4 cup	1 cup
vital gluten, optional	1 tbs.	1 1/2 tbs.	2 tbs.
bread flour	2/3 cup	1 cup	1 1/3 cups
flour equivalents:	*2+ cups*	*3 1/4 cups*	*4 1/3 cups*
cycle:	*whole grain, white, sweet; timer*		
setting:	*medium*		

QUICK SOUR FRENCH

*Light crispy outside with a light fluffy inside. Wonderful! If desired, this may also be made on the dough cycle. See **Shaping and Baking Guidelines**, page 147.*

	Small	Medium	Large
sour cream	½ cup	⅝ cup	¾ cup
milk	½ cup	⅝ cup	¾ cup
vinegar	1 tbs.	1½ tbs.	2 tbs.
sugar	1 tsp.	1½ tsp.	2 tsp.
salt	⅔ tsp.	1 tsp.	1⅓ tsp.
baking soda	⅛ tsp.	⅛+ tsp.	¼ tsp.
bread flour	2 cups	2½ cups	3 cups
yeast	1½ tsp.	2 tsp.	2½ tsp.

flour equivalents: *2 cups*   *2½ cups*   *3 cups*
cycle: *whole grain, sweet, white; no timer (sour cream, milk)*
setting: *light to medium*

REFRIGERATED SOURDOUGH

Wow! This rises and cuts nicely. The starter is moist and sticky when removing it from the pan to refrigerate. The bread has a light, fluffy texture and taste. Good for sandwiches, toast or anything — a versatile bread.

	Small	Medium	Large
starter			
water (100° to 110°)	½ cup	¾ cup	1 cup
bread flour	1 cup	1½ cups	2 cups
vital gluten, optional	1 tsp.	1½ tsp.	2 tsp.
yeast	1 tsp.	1½ tsp.	2 tsp.

Place in machine (any cycle) as usual and allow to knead for 5 to 10 minutes. (Stop machine at that time by using your *stop* or *reset* button or by unplugging.) Dough will be very soft and gooey. Remove from pan and place in a glass bowl, cover with plastic and refrigerate overnight (up to a day and a half is okay). Bring to room temperature prior to starting machine. The dough needs to be watched and more water added if necessary. Start with the amount given and add more, 1 tablespoon at a time, until a soft, round ball is formed.

dough

starter (see previous page)

water	⅓ cup	½ cup	⅔ cup
vegetable oil	1 tbs.	1½ tbs.	2 tbs.
sugar	½ tsp.	¾ tsp.	1 tsp.
salt	⅛ to ⅓ tsp.	¼ to ½ tsp.	⅓ to ¾ tsp.
bread flour	⅔ cup	1 cup	1⅓ cups
oats	⅓ cup	½ cup	⅔ cups
yeast	½ tsp.	1 tsp.	1½ tsp.

flour equivalents:	*2 cups*	*3 cups*	*4 cups*
cycle:	*white; timer*		
setting:	*medium*		

FRUIT BREADS

APPLE CINNAMON BREAD

A delicious breakfast bread. The cinnamon may be increased or decreased to your taste. The applesauce replaces butter or margarine in this recipe. I use frozen apple juice concentrate which has been thawed. A moist texture with light flavor and a crispy crust. Kids love it. Try adding chopped apple (fresh or dried) and nuts.

	Small	Medium	Large
water	½ cup	¾ cup	1 cup
apple juice concentrate	2½ tbs.	3¾ tbs.	5 tbs.
applesauce	¼ cup	⅓ cup	½ cup
cinnamon	½ tsp.	¾ tsp.	1 tsp.
brown sugar	2 tsp.	1 tbs.	1⅓ tbs.
salt	¼ tsp.	⅓ tsp.	½ tsp.
whole wheat flour	1 cup	1½ cups	2 cups
vital gluten, optional	1 to 2 tbs.	1½ to 3 tbs.	2 to 4 tbs.
bread flour	1 cup	1½ cups	2 cups
yeast	1 tsp.	1½ tsp.	2 tsp.
flour equivalents:	*2 cups*	*3 cups*	*4 cups*
cycle:	*white, sweet, whole grain; timer*		
setting:	*medium*		

CRANBERRY ORANGE BREAD

What a festive bread for fall! Use the dried cranberries to enjoy during the rest of the year. An unbeatable combination. Testing was done in the off season using dried cranberries. If using fresh cranberries, they should be finely chopped.

	Small	**Medium**	**Large**
orange juice concentrate	⅓ cup	½ cup	⅔ cup
water	½ cup	¾ cup	1 cup
honey	1 tbs.	1½ tbs.	2 tbs.
salt	¼ tsp.	⅓ tsp.	½ tsp.
whole wheat flour	1 cup	1½ cups	2 cups
bread flour	1 cup	1½ cups	2 cups
yeast	1 tsp.	1½ tsp.	2 tsp.
cranberries	¼ cup	⅓ cup	½ cup
flour equivalents:	*2 cups*	*3 cups*	*4 cups*
cycle:	*raisin/mix; white, sweet*		
setting:	*light to medium*		

PINEAPPLE CRANBERRY BREAD

Nice full-bodied bread with lots of flavor. If desired, add chopped nuts and/or dried cranberries on the raisin/mix cycle. One tester recommended adding coconut flakes in addition to the oats and flour (¼, ⅓ or ½ cup).

	Small	**Medium**	**Large**
cranberry juice	½ cup	¾ cup	1 cup
crushed pineapple	⅓ cup	½ cup	⅔ cup
butter/margarine	1 tbs.	1½ tbs.	2 tbs.
salt	¼ tsp.	⅓ tsp.	½ tsp.
oats	½ cup	¾ cups	1 cup
bread flour	1½ cups	2¼ cups	3 cups
yeast	1 tsp.	1½ tsp.	2 tsp.
flour equivalents:	*2 cups*	*3 cups*	*4 cups*
cycle:	*white, sweet; timer*		
setting:	*light to medium*		

BUTTERMILK BERRY BREAD

A light airy bread with just a hint of berry flavor. Use your favorite berries (strawberries, blueberries, etc.) and process in a food processor or blender until berries are pureed. As with any fruit bread, much of the liquid is derived from the fruit itself, so watch the dough and add more buttermilk or flour if necessary. Serve toasted with cream cheese and berries. If desired, use regular milk cup for cup for the buttermilk and omit the baking soda.

	Small	**Medium**	**Large**
buttermilk	⅓ cup	⅓+ cup	½ cup
berry puree	⅓ cup	⅓+ cup	½ cup
egg	1	1½	2
butter	1 tbs.	1½ tbs.	2 tbs.
sugar	1 tbs.	1½ tbs.	2 tbs.
baking soda	¼ tsp.	⅓ tsp.	½ tsp.
salt	¼ tsp.	⅓ tsp.	½ tsp.
bread flour	2 cups	2½ cups	3 cups
yeast	1 tsp.	1½ tsp.	2 tsp.
flour equivalents:	*2 cups*	*2½ cups*	*3 cups*
cycle:	*white, sweet; no timer (buttermilk, egg)*		
setting:	*light*		

CREAMED CHOCOLATE COCONUT BREAD

A twist on an old favorite. The coconut and oats give the bread a moist, chewy texture. This bread would be a wonderful holiday gift. Four stars!

	Small	Medium	Large
heavy cream	2/3 cup	1 cup	1 1/3 cups
egg	1	1 1/2	2
butter/margarine	2 tbs.	3 tbs.	4 tbs.
sugar	2 tbs.	3 tbs.	1/4 cup
unsweetened cocoa	1 tbs.	1 1/2 tbs.	2 tbs.
salt	1/4 tsp.	1/3 tsp.	1/2 tsp.
coconut flakes	1/4 cup	1/3 cup	1/2 cup
oats	1 cup	1 1/2 cups	2 cups
bread flour	1 cup	1 1/2 cups	2 cups
yeast	1 tsp.	1 1/2 tsp.	2 tsp.
——			
chocolate chips	1/3 cup	1/2 cup	2/3 cup
chopped nuts	1/4 cup	1/3 cup	1/2 cup
flour equivalents:	*2+ cups*	*3+ cups*	*4+ cups*
cycle:	*raisin/mix; white, sweet*		
setting:	*light*		

BLUEBERRY BREAD

This is wonderful! Nice blueberry flavor with a dense texture. Perfect for breakfast or a late morning coffee! Blueberries are pureed by processing in a blender or food processor.

	Small	Medium	Large
blueberry puree	⅔ cup	¾ cup	1 cup
egg	1	1½	2
margarine/butter	2 tbs.	3 tbs.	4 tbs.
sugar	2 tbs.	3 tbs.	¼ cup
salt	¼ tsp.	⅓ tsp.	½ tsp.
bread flour	2 cups	2½ cups	3 cups
yeast	1 tsp.	1½ tsp.	2 tsp.

flour equivalents: *2 cups*   *2½ cups*   *3 cups*
cycle: *white, sweet; no timer (egg)*
setting: *light*

SOUR CREAM LEMON BREAD

*A rich bread with a hint of lemon. Try serving toasted with lemon curd, **Lemon Cream**, page 177 or **Coconut Delight**, page 176, for a delectable treat.*

	Small	**Medium**	**Large**
sour cream	3 tbs.	¼ cup	⅓ cup
milk	⅓ cup	½ cup	⅔ cup
butter/margarine	1½ tbs.	2 tbs.	3 tbs.
eggs	1 small	1	1½
baking soda	⅛+ tsp.	¼ tsp.	⅓ tsp.
grated lemon peel	¼ tsp.	⅓ tsp.	½ tsp.
sugar	1½ tbs.	2 tbs.	3 tbs.
salt	½ tsp.	¾ tsp.	1 tsp.
bread flour	1½ cups	2 cups	3 cups
yeast	1 tsp.	1½ tsp.	2 tsp.

flour equivalents:	*1½ cups*	*2 cups*	*3 cups*
cycle:	*white, sweet; no timer (sour cream, milk, egg)*		
setting:	*light to medium*		

LEMON GINGER BREAD

A light, airy loaf with a delicate taste. The ginger may be increased to taste if desired. A must for lemon lovers!

	Small	**Medium**	**Large**
water	½ cup	⅔ cup	¾ cup
lemon juice	2 tbs.	2½ tbs.	3 tbs.
butter/margarine	2 tbs.	2½ tbs.	3 tbs.
maple syrup	1 tbs.	1¼ tbs.	1½ tbs.
ground ginger	¼ tsp.	⅓ tsp.	½ tsp.
brown sugar	2 tbs.	2½ tbs.	3 tbs.
salt	¼ tsp.	⅓ tsp.	½ tsp.
bread flour	2 cups	2½ cups	3 cups
yeast	1 tsp.	1½ tsp.	2 tsp.
flour equivalent:	*2 cups*	*2½ cups*	*3 cups*
cycle:	*white, sweet; timer*		
setting:	*light to medium*		

CHOCOLATE BANANA BREAD

As with any bread which derives liquid from the fruit, watch the dough and add milk or water, if necessary, one tablespoon at a time, until a nice round ball of dough is formed. The chocolate-banana combo is outstanding. Nuts are optional.

	Small	**Medium**	**Large**
mashed banana	⅔ cup	¾ cup	1 cup
egg	1	1	1½
butter/margarine	2 tbs.	2½ tbs.	3 tbs.
vanilla extract	1 tsp.	1¼ tsp.	1½ tsp.
salt	⅛ tsp.	⅛ tsp.	¼ tsp.
cinnamon	⅓ tsp.	⅓ tsp.	½ tsp.
unsweetened cocoa	1 tbs.	1¼ tbs.	1½ tbs.
sugar	2 tbs.	2½ tbs.	3 tbs.
bread flour	2 cups	2½ cups	3 cups
yeast	1 tsp.	1½ tsp.	2 tsp.
———			
chopped walnuts	2 tbs.	2½ tbs.	3 tbs.

flour equivalents:	*2 cups*	*2½ cups*	*3 cups*
cycle:	*raisin/mix; white, sweet; no timer without nuts (egg)*		
setting:	*light to medium*		

ORANGE GINGER BREAD

This is wonderful! The aroma alone is worth it. A light gingery flavor which is not too sweet.

	Small	Medium	Large
orange juice	2/3 cup	1 cup	1 1/3 cups
butter/margarine	2 tbs.	3 tbs.	4 tbs.
brown sugar	2 tbs.	3 tbs.	1/4 cup
cinnamon	2/3 tsp.	1 tsp.	1 1/3 tsp.
ground ginger	1 tsp.	1 1/2 tsp.	2 tsp.
ground cloves	1/3 tsp.	1/2 tsp.	2/3 tsp.
salt	1/8 tsp.	1/8+ tsp.	1/4 tsp.
bread flour	1 cup	1 1/2 cup	2 cups
whole wheat flour	1 cup	1 1/2 cps	2 cups
yeast	1 tsp.	1 1/2 tsp.	2 tsp.

flour equivalents:	*2 cups*	*3 cups*	*4 cups*
cycle:	*white, sweet; timer*		
setting:	*light to medium*		

GINGER CREAM BREAD

A rich bread with a good creamy flavor. The crystallized ginger should be finely chopped — I use a food processor or blender.

	Small	Medium	Large
cream	2/3 cup	3/4 cup	1 cup
butter	2 tbs.	2½ tbs.	3 tbs.
egg	1	1½	2
vanilla extract	1 tsp.	1¼ tsp.	1½ tsp.
crystallized ginger	1 tbs.	1¼ tbs.	1½ tbs.
brown sugar	1 tbs.	1¼ tbs.	1½ tbs.
salt	¼ tsp.	¼+ tsp.	⅓ tsp.
bread flour	2 cups	2½ cups	3 cups
yeast	1 tsp.	1½ tsp.	2 tsp.

flour equivalents:	*2 cups*	*2½ cups*	*3 cups*
cycle:	*white, sweet; no timer (cream, egg)*		
setting:	*light to medium*		

AMARETTO RAISIN BREAD

A wonderful, light fluffy bread with a crispy crust and a hint of amaretto. Soak raisins in amaretto for approximately one hour and add to your dough at the proper time for your machine.

	Small	**Medium**	**Large**
water	⅔ cup	¾ cup	1 cup
almond extract	⅔ tsp.	¾ tsp.	1 tsp.
vegetable oil	2 tsp.	2½ tsp.	1 tbs.
honey	1 tsp.	1¼ tsp.	1½ tsp.
salt	¼ tsp.	⅓ tsp.	½ tsp.
bread flour	2 cups	2½ cups	3 cups
yeast	1 tsp.	1¼ tsp.	1½ tsp.
amaretto	1 tbs.	1½ tbs.	2 tbs.
raisins	¼ cup	⅓ cup	½ cup
chopped almonds, optional	2 tbs.	2½ tbs.	3 tbs.
flour equivalents:	*2 cups*	*2½ cups*	*3 cups*
cycle:	*raisin/mix; white, sweet*		
setting:	*light to medium*		

CHOCOLATE STRAWBERRY BREAD

Serve this decadent bread with ice cream, fresh strawberries and melted choco-late drizzled on top. Or make French toast and serve with a strawberry syrup and fresh strawberries. Strawberries may be pureed by processing them in a food processor (steel blade) or blender for a minute or two. As with any bread using a fruit as part of the liquid, watch the dough and add water if necessary.

	Small	Medium	Large
strawberry puree	2/3 cup	7/8 cup	1 cup
butter	2 tbs.	2½ tbs.	3 tbs.
sugar	2 tbs.	2½ tbs.	3 tbs.
unsweetened cocoa	1 tbs.	1¼ tbs.	1½ tbs.
salt	¼ tsp.	⅓ tsp.	½ tsp.
bread flour	2 cups	2½ cups	3 cups
yeast	1 tsp.	1½ tsp.	2 tsp.
chocolate chips	⅓ cup	½ cup	⅔ cup
flour equivalents:	*2 cups*	*2½ cups*	*3 cups*
cycle:	*raisin/mix; white, sweet*		
setting:	*light*		

BIMINI (COCONUT) BREAD

Based on a recipe given to me by my father-in-law, a (rare) native Floridian. This is an outstanding bread — great with coffee or alone as a snack. Mary Vollendorf adds more coconut flakes, white chocolate chips and chopped nuts to this (a few tablespoons of each). This works great in some machines, but not those which are prone to "doughy blues."

	Small	Medium	Large
milk	⅔ cup	¾ cup	1 cup
coconut extract	2 tsp.	2½ tsp.	1 tbs.
butter/margarine	1 tbs.	1¼ tbs.	1½ tbs.
egg	1	1	1½
sugar	2 tbs.	2½ tbs.	3 tbs.
salt	¼ to ½ tsp.	⅓ to ⅔ tsp.	½ to 1 tsp.
coconut flakes	¼ cup	¼+ cup	⅓ cup
bread flour	2 cups	2½ cups	3 cups
yeast	1 tsp.	1½ tsp.	2 tsp.
flour equivalents:	*2 cups*	*2½ cups*	*3 cups*
cycle:	*white, sweet; no timer (milk, egg)*		
setting:	*light*		

LEMON SAFFRON BREAD

*A distinctive tasting bread with a wonderful yellow color. Serve with lemon curd or any of the wonderful lemon toppings (see **Toppings**, page 166).*

	Small	Medium	Large
water/milk	¾ cup	1⅛ cups	1½ cups
lemon juice concentrate	1 tbs.	1⅓ tbs.	1½ tbs.
sugar	2 tbs.	2½ tbs.	3 tbs.
salt	¼ tsp.	⅓ tsp.	½ tsp.
lemon peel	¼ tsp.	⅓ tsp.	⅓+ tsp.
ground saffron	⅛ tsp.	⅛+ tsp.	¼ tsp.
bread flour	2 cups	2½ cups	3 cups
yeast	1 tsp.	1½ tsp.	2 tsp.

flour equivalents:	*2 cups*	*2½ cups*	*3 cups*
cycle:	*white, sweet; timer with water*		
setting:	*light to medium*		

PUMPKIN APPLE BREAD

Who could ask for a better bread to enjoy on a nice fall day? The pumpkin pie spice may be adjusted to taste. For a delectable treat, try this as a sandwich bread with cream cheese and apple or pumpkin butter. Dried apple and nuts are optional.

	Small	Medium	Large
apple juice	¼ cup	⅓ cup	½ cup
pumpkin	⅔ cup	1 cup	1⅓ cups
apple juice concentrate	1 tbs.	1½ tbs.	2 tbs.
brown/maple sugar	2 tbs.	3 tbs.	¼ cup
pumpkin pie spice	1 tsp.	1½ tsp.	2 tsp.
salt	⅓ tsp.	¼ tsp.	⅔ tsp.
oats	½ cup	¾ cup	1 cup
bread flour	1½ cups	2¼ cups	3 cups
yeast	1 tsp.	1½ tsp.	2 tsp.
dried apple, diced	¼ cup	⅓ cup	½ cup
ground nuts	2 tbs.	3 tbs.	¼ cup
flour equivalents:	*2 cups*	*3 cups*	*4 cups*
cycle:	*raisin/mix; white, sweet; timer if no apple, nuts*		
setting:	*light to medium*		

IRISH SODA BREAD

Bettie Cooper has adapted this recipe to her bread machine and says it is a favorite with all of her friends. It is required that she take it to any get-togethers.

	Small	Medium	Large
vinegar	1 tbs.	1¼ tbs.	1½ tbs.
skim milk*	1 cup	1¼ cups	1½ cups
canola oil	1 tbs.	1¼ tbs.	1½ tbs.
raisins	¼ cup	5 tbs.	⅓ cup
sugar	2 tbs.	2½ tbs.	3 tbs.
salt	⅔ tsp.	¾ tsp.	1 tsp.
caraway seeds	2 tbs.	2½ tbs.	3 tbs.
bread flour	1¼ cups	1⅔ cups	1⅞ cups
whole wheat flour	1 cup	1¼ cups	1½ cups
yeast	1½ tsp.	2 tsp.	2½ tsp.
raisins	⅓ cup	½ cup	⅔ cups

*Measure the vinegar into your liquid measuring cup. Add skim milk. Or substitute fresh buttermilk for vinegar and skim milk.

flour equivalents:	*2¼ cups*	*2⅞ cups*	*3⅜ cups*
cycle:	*raisin/mix; sweet*		
setting:	*light to medium*		

SWEET RAISIN BREAD

Gold raisins tend to be sweeter than the darker ones. You may use whichever ones you prefer. This dough is very liquid which results in an extremely light, high-rising loaf. The raisins may be increased if your machine has no problems cooking fruited loaves completely.

	Small	Medium	Large
milk/water	2/3 cup	1 cup	1 1/3 cup
butter/margarine	1 tbs.	1 1/2 tbs.	2 tbs.
sugar	1 1/2 tbs.	2 1/3 tbs.	3 tbs.
salt	1/2 tsp.	2/3 tsp.	1 tsp.
grated lemon peel	1/2 tsp.	3/4 tsp.	1 tsp.
bread flour	1 1/2 cups	2 1/4 cups	3 cups
yeast	1 tsp.	1 1/2 tsp.	2 tsp.
golden raisins	1/3 cup	1/2 cup	2/3 cup
chopped nuts, optional	1/4 cup	1/3 cup	1/2 cup

flour equivalents: 1 1/2 cups | 2 1/4 cups | 3 cups
cycle: white, sweet; timer with water
setting: light

POPPY SEED BREAD

*Poppy seeds are a favorite in everything from cakes to bread. Unlimited versions abound — here's another one to enjoy. Poppy seeds may be purchased in bulk (much more economical) from mail order catalogs (see **Sources**, page 183) or gourmet shops.*

	Small	**Medium**	**Large**
milk	2/3 cup	3/4 cup	1 cup
butter/margarine	2 tbs.	2½ tbs.	3 tbs.
salt	2/3 tsp.	3/4 tsp.	1 tsp.
lemon peel, optional	1 tsp.	1¼ tsp.	1½ tsp.
sugar	2 tbs.	2½ tbs.	3 tbs.
poppy seeds	2 tbs.	2½ tbs.	3 tbs.
bread flour	2 cups	2½ cups	3 cups
yeast	1 tsp.	1½ tsp.	2 tsp.

flour equivalents:	*2 cups*	*2½ cups*	*3 cups*
cycle:	*white, sweet; no timer (milk)*		
setting:	*light*		

PRUNE BREAD

Priscilla Ward of Delaware shares her favorite bread which she developed using her bread machine. She says that she snips each prune into 8 pieces — I let the machine mash them for me! I also cut back on the amount of juice she uses.

	Small	**Medium**	**Large**
cran-raspberry juice	¾ cup	1 cup	1½ cups
margarine/butter	1¼ tbs.	1⅔ tbs.	2½ tbs.
sugar	1½ tbs.	2¼ tbs.	3 tbs.
salt	½ tsp.	¾ tsp.	1 tsp.
whole wheat flour	½ cup	¾ cup	1 cup
bread flour	1½ cups	2¼ cups	3 cups
yeast	1 tsp.	1½ tsp.	2 tsp.
───			
snipped pitted prunes	⅓ to ½ cup	½ to ⅔ cup	⅔ to ¾ cup

flour equivalents:	*2 cups*	*3 cups*	*4 cups*
cycle:	*raisin/mix, sweet, white*		
setting:	*light to medium*		

SQUAW BREAD

Karen Pennington adapted this version of an often requested bread for the bread machines. A nice, sweet bread. Karen mixes the first five ingredients together in a blender until liquified; I simply put them in all at once and let the machine mash the raisins! A few tablespoons of sunflower seeds may be added for variation.

	Small	Medium	Large
water	2/3 cup	1⅛ cups	1⅓ cups
vegetable oil	1⅓ tbs.	2 tbs.	2⅔ tbs.
honey	1 tbs.	1½ tbs.	2 tbs.
brown/maple sugar	1 tbs.	1½ tbs.	2 tbs.
raisins	1 tbs.	1½ tbs.	2 tbs.
salt	½ to ⅔ tsp.	⅔ to 1 tsp.	1 to 1½ tsp.
rye flour	½ cup	¾ cup	1 cup
whole wheat flour	½ cup	¾ cup	1 cup
bread flour	1 cup	1½ cups	2 cups
yeast	1½ tsp.	2 tsp.	2½ tsp.
flour equivalents:	*2 cups*	*3 cups*	*4 cups*
cycle:	*white, sweet; timer*		
setting:	*light to medium*		

ORANGE SHERRY RAISIN BREAD

The raisins are plumped in sherry for a tasty treat and are still fat and juicy after baking! The orange peel really gives this "zing!" Great with cream cheese. Soak the raisins in the sherry overnight or for at least 6 to 8 hours. When starting the dough, drain the sherry into the pan with the other liquid ingredients.

	Small	Medium	Large
orange juice	⅔ cup	1 cup	1⅓ cups
vegetable oil	2 tbs.	3 tbs.	¼ cup
honey	2 tbs.	3 tbs.	¼ cup
orange peel	⅓ tsp.	½ tsp.	⅔ tsp.
whole wheat flour	1 cup	1½ cups	2 cups
bread flour	1 cup	1½ cups	2 cups
yeast	1 tsp.	1½ tsp.	2 tsp.
———			
dry sherry	2 tbs.	3 tbs.	¼ cup
raisins	⅓ cup	½ cup	⅔ cup

flour equivalents:	*2 cups*	*3 cups*	*4 cups*
cycle:	*raisin/mix; white, sweet*		
setting:	*light to medium*		

APRICOT CORNMEAL BREAD

What a combination — sure to please the apricot lover in your family. A true winner!

	Small	**Medium**	**Large**
milk/water	⅔ cup	1 cup	1⅓ cups
apricot nectar	1 tbs.	1½ tbs.	2 tbs.
honey	1 tbs.	1½ tbs.	2 tbs.
salt	⅔ tsp.	1 tsp.	1⅓ tsp.
cornmeal	½ cup	¾ cup	1 cup
bread flour	1½ cups	2¼ cups	3 cups
yeast	1 tsp.	1½ tsp.	2 tsp.
diced dried apricots	¼ cup	⅓ cup	½ cup

flour equivalents:	*2 cups*	*3 cups*	*4 cups*
cycle:	*raisin/mix; white, sweet*		
setting:	*light to medium*		

BANANA AMARANTH BREAD

Amaranth is a great source of protein and combines nicely with banana in this loaf. If necessary, add water to mashed banana to equal amount in recipe. Watch the kneading of the dough and add water, 1 tbs. at a time until ball is formed.

	Small	Medium	Large
milk	⅔ cup	1 cup	1⅓ cups
mashed banana	¼ cup	⅓ cup	½ cup
walnut oil	2 tsp.	1 tbs.	1⅓ tbs.
honey	2 tbs.	3 tbs.	¼ cup
salt	¼ tsp.	⅓ tsp.	½ tsp.
cinnamon	⅛ tsp.	⅛+ tsp.	¼ tsp.
amaranth flour	¼ cup	⅓ cup	½ cup
whole wheat flour	½ cup	¾ cup	1 cup
vital gluten, optional	1 tbs.	1½ tbs.	2 tbs.
bread flour	1¼ cups	1⅔ cups	2½ cups
yeast	1½ tsp.	2 tsp.	2½ tsp.
chopped nuts, optional	¼ cup	⅓ cup	½ cup
flour equivalents:	*2 cups*	*3 cups*	*4 cups*
cycle:	*raisin/mix; white, sweet; no timer without nuts (milk)*		
setting:	*medium*		

FRUIT COCKTAIL BREAD

The coconut flakes really add that special touch to this bread. Serve this toasted with ice cream and coconut flakes for a different dessert treat. Do not drain the fruit cocktail.

	Small	Medium	Large
fruit cocktail	3/4 cup	1 1/8 cups	1 1/2 cups
vegetable oil	1 tbs.	1 1/2 tbs.	2 tbs.
fruit juice concentrate	2 tbs.	3 tbs.	1/4 cup
salt	1/4 tsp.	1/3 tsp.	1/2 tsp.
coconut flakes	1/4 cup	1/3 cup	1/2 cup
whole wheat flour	1 cup	1 1/2 cups	2 cups
bread flour	1 cup	1 1/2 cups	2 cups
yeast	1 tsp.	1 1/2 tsp.	2 tsp.

flour equivalents:	*2 cups*	*3 cups*	*4 cups*
cycle:	*white, sweet; timer*		
setting:	*light to medium*		

ORANGE RYE CORNMEAL BREAD

A tasty but very low-rising loaf of bread. The combination is unbeatable! Tip: 1⅞ cups equals 2 cups less 2 tbs.

	Small	**Medium**	**Large**
orange juice	¾ cup	1⅛ cups	1½ cups
orange juice concentrate	2 tbs.	3 tbs.	¼ cup
honey	1 tbs.	1½ tbs.	2 tbs.
salt	⅓ tsp.	½ tsp.	⅔ tsp.
vital gluten	1 to 2 tbs.	1½ to 3 tbs.	2 to 4 tbs.
cornmeal	½ cup	¾ cup	1 cup
rye flour	¼ cup	⅓ cup	½ cup
bread flour	1¼ cups	1⅞ cups	2½ cups
yeast	1 tsp.	1½ tsp.	2 tsp.

flour equivalents:	*2 cups*	*3 cups*	*4 cups*
cycle:	*whole grain, white, sweet; timer*		
setting:	*medium*		

CHOCOLATE CHOCOLATE CHIP BREAD

For all the chocoholics of the world! A good chocolate flavor without being too sweet. One tester replaced the sugar with date sugar and highly recommends it.

	Small	**Medium**	**Large**
milk	½ cup	¾ cup	1 cup
margarine/butter	1 tbs.	1½ tbs.	2 tbs.
eggs	1	1½	2
vanilla extract	1 tsp.	1½ tsp.	2 tsp.
sugar	2 tbs.	3 tbs.	4 tbs.
unsweetened cocoa	1 tbs.	1½ tbs.	2 tbs.
salt	¼ tsp.	⅓ tsp.	½ tsp.
bread flour	1½ cups	2¼ cups	3 cups
yeast	1 tsp.	1½ tsp.	2 tsp.
-----			
chocolate chips	¼ to ⅓ cup	⅓ to ½ cup	½ to ⅔ cup

flour equivalents:	*1½ cups*	*2¼ cups*	*3 cups*
cycle:	*raisin/mix; sweet, white*		
setting:	*light to medium*		

CHOCOLATE CHIP BANANA COCONUT BREAD

A flavorful sweet bread which could be served for brunch or dessert with ice cream. The chips may become mashed in the bread which gives it a chocolate appearance instead of the visible chips. Either way, it is just as good.

	Small	Medium	Large
milk	½ cup	¾ cup	1 cup
mashed banana	¼ cup	⅓ cup	½ cup
butter/margarine	1 tbs.	1½ tbs.	2 tbs.
sugar	1 tbs.	1½ tbs.	2 tbs.
salt	¼ tsp.	⅓ tsp.	½ tsp.
coconut flakes	¼ cup	⅓ cup	½ cup
bread flour	1½ cups	2¼ cups	3 cups
oats	½ cup	¾ cup	1 cup
yeast	1 tsp.	1½ tsp.	2 tsp.
chocolate chips	¼ cup	⅓ cup	½ cup
flour equivalents:	*2 cups*	*3 cups*	*4 cups*
cycle:	*raisin/mix; white, sweet*		
setting:	*light to medium*		

ORANGE BOURBON BREAD

A great holiday and gift bread. Soak raisins in bourbon for 30 minutes or longer prior to starting the machine. Pour off any excess liquid and add to other liquid ingredients; add raisins at the normal time. Try freshly grated nutmeg — much better!

	Small	Medium	Large
bourbon	2 tbs.	3 tbs.	¼ cup
orange juice	½ cup	¾ cup	1 cup
eggs	1	1½	2
butter/margarine	2 tbs.	3 tbs.	4 tbs.
sugar	2 tbs.	3 tbs.	4 tbs.
salt	¼ tsp.	⅓ tsp.	½ tsp.
nutmeg	⅛ tsp.	⅛+ tsp.	¼ tsp.
bread flour	1 cup	1½ cups	2 cups
whole wheat flour	1 cup	1½ cups	2 cups
yeast	1 tsp.	1½ tsp.	2 tsp.
raisins	⅓ cup	½ cup	⅔ cup
bourbon	2 tbs.	3 tbs.	¼ cup
flour equivalent:	*2 cups*	*3 cups*	*4 cups*
cycle:	*raisin/mix, sweet, white*		
setting:	*light to medium*		

ORANGE COTTAGE CHEESE BREAD

Great taste and texture on this low-rising bread. Allow the dough to knead for at least 5 minutes before looking to see if added liquid (orange segments) are required. I use canned mandarin orange segments which have been drained. Try this toasted with orange marmalade!

	Small	**Medium**	**Large**
orange segments	½ cup	¾ cup	1 cup
cottage cheese	¼ cup	⅓ cup	½ cup
vegetable oil	1 tbs.	1½ tbs.	2 tbs.
honey	1 tbs.	1½ tbs.	2 tbs.
salt	¼ tsp.	⅓ tsp.	½ tsp.
baking soda	¼ tsp.	⅓ tsp.	½ tsp.
oats	½ cup	¾ cup	1 cup
bread flour	1½ cups	2¼ cups	3 cups
yeast	1 tsp.	1½ tsp.	2 tsp.

flour equivalents:	*2 cups*	*3 cups*	*4 cups*
cycle:	*white, sweet; no timer (cottage cheese)*		
setting:	*light to medium*		

HERB AND SPICE BREADS

Herbs and spices add zest and flavor to all foods, including bread. Recipes in this section use dried herbs (such as found in the spice section of the grocery store). If fresh herbs are available, simply triple the amount given in the recipe. You may prefer to adjust the herbs or spices to your taste.

Spices are obtained from either the bark, root, fruit or berry of plants and are used ground or whole, such as allspice, cinnamon, cloves, ginger, nutmeg, paprika, lemon or orange peels and vanilla beans.

Herbs are plant leaves which are crushed, such as basil, bay leaves, dill weed, mint, oregano, parsley, sage, rosemary and thyme.

OREGANO BREAD - NO CHEESE

Due to so many requests for reduced fat, I have revised one of our all-time favorites. Fructose may be used in place of the sugar if the amount is cut to: 1, 1¼ or 2 tsp. Basil or another favorite herb may be substituted for the oregano. This flavorful bread is terrific with lasagna or a similar meal.

	Small	**Medium**	**Large**
water	⅔ cup	¾ cup	1 cup
olive oil	1 tbs.	1½ tbs.	2 tbs.
egg	1	1	1½
sugar	1 tbs.	1⅓ tbs.	1½ tbs.
salt	¼ to ⅓ tsp.	⅓ to ½ tsp.	½ to ⅔ tsp.
oregano	1 tbs.	1½ tbs.	2 tbs.
bread flour	2 cups	2½ cups	3 cups
yeast	1 tsp.	1½ tsp.	2 tsp.

flour equivalents:	*2 cups*	*2½ cups*	*3 cups*
cycle:	*white; no timer (egg)*		
setting:	*medium*		

GINGER BREAD

A wonderful aroma fills the house while this bakes and the taste is just as good!

	Small	**Medium**	**Large**
buttermilk	3/4 cup	1 1/8 cups	1 1/2 cups
vegetable oil	1 tbs.	1 1/2 tbs.	2 tbs.
molasses	1 tbs.	1 1/2 tbs.	2 tbs.
egg	1	1 1/2	2
salt	1/3 tsp.	1/2 tsp.	2/3 tsp.
baking soda	1/4 tsp.	1/3 tsp.	1/2 tsp.
ground ginger	1 tsp.	1 1/2 tsp.	2 tsp.
cinnamon	1 tsp.	1 1/2 tsp.	2 tsp.
ground cloves	1/3 tsp.	1/2 tsp.	2/3 tsp.
nutmeg	1/3 tsp.	1/2 tsp.	2/3 tsp.
orange peel	1/4 tsp.	1/3 tsp.	1/2 tsp.
bread flour	1 cup	1 1/2 cups	2 cups
whole wheat flour	1 cup	1 1/2 cups	2 cups
yeast	1 tsp.	1 1/2 tsp.	2 tsp.

flour equivalents: *2 cups*   *3 cups*   *4 cups*
cycle: *white, sweet; no timer (buttermilk, egg)*
setting: *light to medium*

CAYENNE CORN BREAD

A hot, spicy cornbread with a consistency similar to corn muffins.

	Small	**Medium**	**Large**
milk/water	¾ cup	1⅛ cups	1½ cups
margarine/butter	1 tbs.	1½ tbs.	2 tbs.
brown sugar	1 tbs.	1½ tbs.	2 tbs.
salt	⅛ tsp.	⅛+ tsp.	¼ tsp.
cayenne pepper	½ tsp.	¾ tsp.	1 tsp.
cornmeal	½ cup	¾ cup	1 cup
bread flour	1½ cups	2¼ cups	3 cups
yeast	1 tsp.	1½ tsp.	2 tsp.

flour equivalents:	*2 cups*	*3 cups*	*4 cups*
cycle:	*white, sweet; timer with water*		
setting:	*medium*		

MEXICAN CORN BREAD

Wow!! This will soon become a favorite in your house too. I ran out of creamed corn during my testing once so I filled my measuring cup with thawed frozen corn and then poured in milk to top it off — worked great. Both the corn and the salsa can throw off the liquid/flour ratio, so check the dough about 3 to 5 minutes into the kneading and add more water or flour as necessary.

	Small	Medium	Large
creamed corn	2/3 cup	1 cup	1 1/3 cups
vegetable oil	1 tbs.	1 1/2 tbs.	2 tbs.
honey	2 tsp.	1 tbs.	1 1/3 tbs.
grated cheddar	1/4 cup	1/3 cup	1/2 cup
salsa	1/4 cup	1/3 cup	1/2 cup
salt	1/3 tsp.	1/2 tsp.	2/3 tsp.
cornmeal	1/2 cup	3/4 cup	1 cup
bread flour	1 1/2 cups	2 1/4 cups	3 cups
yeast	1 tsp.	1 1/2 tsp.	2 tsp.

flour equivalents:	*2 cups*	*3 cups*	*4 cups*
cycle:	*white, sweet; no timer (creamed corn)*		
setting:	*light to medium*		

HERB CORN BREAD

A delightful, flavorful bread to serve with chicken and a green salad or a Mexican-style dinner. It is also good toasted with honey! For variety, try omitting the three herbs and using paprika (1 tsp., 1½ tsp., 2 tsp.).

	Small	Medium	Large
milk/water	¾ cup	1⅛ cups	1½ cups
vegetable oil	1 tbs.	1½ tbs.	2 tbs.
honey/maple syrup	1 tbs.	1½ tbs.	2 tbs.
salt	¼ tsp.	⅓ tsp.	½ tsp.
thyme	¼ tsp.	⅓ tsp.	½ tsp.
oregano	¼ tsp.	⅓ tsp.	½ tsp.
celery seeds	⅛ tsp.	⅛+ tsp.	¼ tsp.
cornmeal	½ cup	¾ cup	1 cup
bread flour	1½ cups	2¼ cups	3 cups
yeast	1 tsp.	1½ tsp.	2 tsp.

flour equivalents:	*2 cups*	*3 cups*	*4 cups*
cycle:	*white, sweet; timer with water*		
setting:	*light to medium*		

CORNMEAL CHEESE BREAD

This hearty loaf is great with a Mexican dish. The cheese adds wonderful flavor to cornmeal. Try serving this toasted, topped with melted cheese and salsa!

	Small	Medium	Large
buttermilk	3/4 cup	1 1/8 cups	1 1/2 cups
grated cheese	1/3 cup	1/2 cup	2/3 cup
butter/margarine	1 tbs.	1 1/2 tbs.	2 tbs.
baking soda	1/4 tsp.	1/3 tsp.	1/2 tsp.
sugar	1 tbs.	1 1/2 tbs.	2 tbs.
salt	1/4 tsp.	1/3 tsp.	1/2 tsp.
caraway seeds	1 tsp.	1 1/2 tsp.	2 tsp.
cornmeal	1/2 cup	3/4 cup	1 cup
bread flour	1 1/2 cups	2 1/4 cups	3 cups
yeast	1 tsp.	1 1/2 tsp.	2 tsp.

flour equivalents: *2 cups*   *3 cups*   *4 cups*
cycle: *white, sweet; no timer (buttermilk)*
setting: *light to medium*

HUNGARIAN ONION BREAD

Paprika adds both flavor and color to this wonderful, aromatic onion bread. Serve with cream cheese as an appetizer or toast slices of this bread on the grill and serve with hamburgers for a delightful change from buns. Liquid is provided by the diced onion; watch the dough and add more water if necessary to form a well-rounded ball of dough.

	Small	**Medium**	**Large**
water	½ cup	⅔ cup	¾ cup
butter/margarine	1 tbs.	1¼ tbs.	1½ tbs.
finely diced onion	¼ cup	¼+ cup	⅓ cup
sugar	½ tsp.	⅔ tsp.	¾ tsp.
salt	⅛ tsp.	⅛+ tsp.	¼ tsp.
paprika	⅔ tsp.	¾ tsp.	1 tsp.
bread flour	2 cups	2½ cups	3 cups
yeast	1 tsp.	1½ tsp.	2 tsp.
flour equivalents:	*2 cups*	*2½ cups*	*3 cups*
cycle:	*white; timer*		
setting:	*medium*		

HERB SALLY LUNN

A nice variation on a plain Sally Lunn. Oregano or rosemary may be used as well, if desired. Evaporated skim milk may be substituted for the cream if counting calories.

	Small	Medium	Large
heavy cream	½ cup	5⁄8 cup	¾ cup
milk	¼ cup	3⁄8 cup	⅓ cup
eggs	1	1½	2
butter/margarine	2 tbs.	2½ tbs.	3 tbs.
sugar	2 tbs.	2½ tbs.	3 tbs.
salt	½ tsp.	¾ tsp.	1 tsp.
basil	1 tsp.	1¼ tsp.	1½ tsp.
bread flour	2 cups	2½ cups	3 cups
yeast	1 tsp.	1½ tsp.	2 tsp.

flour equivalents:	*2 cups*	*2½ cups*	*3 cups*
cycle:	*white, sweet; no timer (cream, milk, egg)*		
setting:	*light to medium*		

DILL PARSLEY BREAD

Heather Smith adapted this favorite recipe for her bread machine. Wonderful served with turkey or chicken.

	Small	**Medium**	**Large**
water	⅔ cup	¾ cup	1 cup
olive oil	¼ cup	¼+ cup	⅓ cup
sugar	½ tsp.	⅔ tsp.	¾ tsp.
salt	¼ tsp.	⅓ tsp.	½ tsp.
parsley	1 tbs.	1⅓ tbs.	1½ tbs.
dill weed	1 tbs.	1⅓ tbs.	1½ tbs.
bread flour	2 cups	2½ cups	3 cups
nonfat dry milk	3 tbs.	¼ cup	5 tbs.
yeast	1½ tsp.	2 tsp.	2½ tsp.
flour equivalents:	*2 cups*	*2½ cups*	*3 cups*
cycle:	*white; timer*		
setting:	*medium*		

SCALLION SESAME BREAD

Serve this interesting, Oriental-flavored bread with a curry chicken or similar meal. For a real twist, try adding raisins (1/4, 1/3 or 1/2 cup). The loaf is low-rising with a heavy texture which cuts nicely.

	Small	Medium	Large
milk	3/4 cup	1 1/8 cups	1 1/2 cups
sesame oil	1/2 tsp.	3/4 tsp.	1 tsp.
scallions, chopped	1/4 cup	1/3 cup	1/2 cup
brown sugar	1/4 tsp.	1/3 tsp.	1/2 tsp.
sesame seeds	2 tsp.	1 tbs.	1 1/3 tbs.
salt	1/8 tsp.	1/8+ tsp.	1/4 tsp.
garlic powder	1/8 tsp.	1/8+ tsp.	1/4 tsp.
whole wheat flour	1 cup	1 1/2 cups	2 cups
bread flour	1 cup	1 1/2 cups	2 cups
yeast	1 tsp.	1 1/2 tsp.	2 tsp.
flour equivalents:	*2 cups*	*3 cups*	*4 cups*
cycle:	*white; no timer (milk)*		
setting:	*medium*		

SESAME ONION CHEESE BREAD

A beautiful loaf with nice hearty Oriental flavor. I like using a sharp cheddar in this recipe.

	Small	Medium	Large
milk	⅔ cup	1 cup	1⅓ cups
diced onion	¼ cup	⅓ cup	½ cup
grated cheese	⅓ cup	½ cup	⅔ cup
butter/margarine	1 tbs.	1½ tbs.	2 tbs.
sugar	1 tbs.	1½ tbs.	2 tbs.
salt	⅓ tsp.	½ tsp.	⅔ tsp.
sesame seeds	2 tsp.	1 tbs.	1⅓ tbs.
whole wheat flour	1 cup	1½ cups	2 cups
bread flour	1 cup	1½ cups	2 cups
yeast	1 tsp.	1½ tsp.	2 tsp.
flour equivalents:	*2 cups*	*3 cups*	*4 cups*
cycle:	*white, sweet; no timer (milk, cheese)*		
setting:	*medium*		

TURKEY STUFFING BREAD

Joan Garneau makes this bread just to stuff turkey with, or to serve as a dressing on the side with a turkey breast. The bread is a treat as is, too!

	Small	Medium	Large
water	2/3 cup	1 cup	1 1/3 cups
egg	1 small	1 large	2 small
butter/margarine	2 tbs.	3 tbs.	4 tbs.
diced onion	1/4 cup	1/3 cup	1/2 cup
brown/white sugar	1 1/2 tsp.	2 1/4 tsp.	1 tbs.
salt	1/3 tsp.	1/2 tsp.	2/3 tsp.
black pepper (coarse)	1/4 tsp.	1/3 tsp.	1/2 tsp.
dry sage	2/3 tsp.	1 tsp.	1 1/3 tsp.
celery seeds	2/3 tsp.	1 tsp.	1 1/3 tsp.
poultry seasoning	1/2 tsp.	3/4 tsp.	1 tsp.
cornmeal	1/2 cup	2/3 cup	1 cup
bread flour	1 2/3 cups	2 1/2 cups	3 1/3 cups
yeast	1 tsp.	1 1/2 tsp.	2 tsp.
flour equivalents:	*2+ cups*	*3+ cups*	*4 1/3 cups*
cycle:	*white, sweet; no timer (egg)*		
setting:	*medium*		

FAVORITE FENNEL BREAD

A light fluffy texture with the great flavor of fennel; adjust amounts to taste.

	Small	Medium	Large
milk/water	3/4 cup	1 cup	1 1/8 cups
butter/margarine	1 tbs.	1 1/3 tbs.	1 1/2 tbs.
sugar	1 tbs.	1 1/3 tbs.	1 1/2 tbs.
baking soda	1/4 tsp.	1/3 tsp.	1/2 tsp.
salt	1/4 tsp.	1/3 tsp.	1/2 tsp.
fennel seeds	1 tsp.	1 1/2 tsp.	2 tsp.
bread flour	2 cups	2 1/2 cups	3 cups
yeast	1 tsp.	1 1/2 tsp.	2 tsp.

flour equivalents:	*2 cups*	*2 1/2 cups*	*3 cups*
cycle:	*white, sweet; timer with water*		
setting:	*medium*		

GOLDEN CHEESE BREAD

This is out of this world — an absolute "must try." The combination of cheeses and herbs is unbeatable. Four stars!

	Small	**Medium**	**Large**
buttermilk	2/3 cup	1 cup	1 1/3 cups
butter/margarine	1 tbs.	1 1/2 tbs.	2 tbs.
egg	1	1 1/2	2
grated cheddar	1/4 cup	1/3 cup	1/2 cup
crumbled blue cheese	2 tbs.	3 tbs.	1/4 cup
salt	1/4 tsp.	1/3 tsp.	1/2 tsp.
coarse black pepper	1/8 tsp.	1/8+ tsp.	1/4 tsp.
caraway seeds	1 tsp.	1 1/2 tsp.	2 tsp.
wheat/oat flakes	1/2 cup	3/4 cup	1 cup
bread flour	1 1/2 cups	2 1/4 cups	3 cups
yeast	1 tsp.	1 1/2 tsp.	2 tsp.

flour equivalents: *2 cups   3 cups   4 cups*
cycle: *white, sweet; no timer (buttermilk, egg)*
setting: *light to medium*

PEPPERONI BREAD

Ann Goss makes this bread for a friend who loves pizza. Good alone, or layer a slice of mozzarella cheese, pizza sauce and any other desired ingredients on top of a slice of this bread. Pop it under the broiler just to melt the cheese and heat. The pepperoni should have the skin removed and be ground or diced in a food processor and added at the beginning so that it is evenly distributed. Premixed Italian spices or oregano or basil may be added to taste if desired (½ to 2 tsp.)

	Small	Medium	Large
water/milk	¾ cup	1⅛ cups	1½ cups
olive oil/butter	1 tbs.	1½ tbs.	2 tbs.
pepperoni	3 oz.	4½ oz.	6 oz.
sugar	2 tbs.	3 tbs.	¼ cup
Italian spices, optional	to taste	to taste	to taste
salt	½ tsp.	¾ tsp.	1 tsp.
bread flour	1 cup	1½ cups	2 cups
whole wheat flour	1 cup	1½ cups	2 cups
yeast	1½ tsp.	2 tsp.	2½ tsp.
flour equivalents:	*2 cups*	*3 cups*	*4 cups*
cycle:	*white, sweet; timer with water*		
setting:	*medium*		

ITALIAN HERB BREAD

A light loaf which is out of this world. For variation, try substituting rosemary for the basil. The recipe upon which this was based called for gold raisins which are sweeter than the dark ones. Use whichever raisins you wish — both are good.

	Small	**Medium**	**Large**
water	2⁄3 cup	1 cup	1 1⁄3 cups
olive oil	1 tbs.	1 1⁄2 tbs.	2 tbs.
sugar	2 tsp.	1 tbs.	1 1⁄3 tbs.
salt	1⁄3 tsp.	1⁄2 tsp.	2⁄3 tsp.
basil	1⁄2 tsp.	3⁄4 tsp.	1 tsp.
raisins	1 to 2 tbs.	1 1⁄2 to 3 tbs.	2 to 4 tbs.
bread flour	1 1⁄2 cups	2 1⁄4 cups	3 cups
yeast	1 tsp.	1 1⁄2 tsp.	2 tsp.

flour equivalents:	*1 1⁄2 cups*	*2 1⁄4 cups*	*3 cups*
cycle:	*white, sweet; timer*		
setting:	*light to medium*		

TOMATO HERB BREAD

Carol Ashman of California developed this recipe when looking for something to do with the juice and seeds from garden tomatoes she was drying. She also uses fresh herbs from her garden. For those of us who don't have fresh, chopped herbs, simply substitute dried herbs (⅓ the amount listed). The tomato juice is the juice and seeds taken from fresh tomatoes; water may be added if necessary. If using canned tomato juice which contains salt, delete the salt from the recipe.

	Small	**Medium**	**Large**
tomato juice	¾ cup	1 cup	1⅛ cups
vegetable oil	1 tbs.	2⅔ tbs.	3 tbs.
sugar	1 tbs.	1⅓ tbs.	1½ tbs.
tarragon or basil	1½ tbs.	2 tbs.	2⅓ tbs.
salt	½ tsp.	⅔ tsp.	¾ tsp.
bread flour	2 cups	2⅔ cups	3 cups
yeast	1 tsp.	1½ tsp.	2 tsp.

flour equivalents:	*2 cups*	*2⅔ cups*	*3 cups*
cycle:	*white, sweet*		
setting:	*medium*		

NUT BREADS

MAPLE WALNUT BREAD

Wow! It is worth buying walnut oil to enjoy in this nutty tasting bread. Of course, any vegetable oil may be substituted but will not have quite the flavor.

	Small	**Medium**	**Large**
water	¾ cup	1⅛ cups	1½ cups
walnut oil	1 tbs.	1½ tbs.	2 tbs.
maple syrup	2 tbs.	3 tbs.	¼ cup
cinnamon	⅛ tsp.	⅛+ tsp.	¼ tsp.
salt	¼ tsp.	⅓ tsp.	½ tsp.
whole wheat	1 cup	1½ cups	2 cups
bread flour	1 cup	1½ cups	2 cups
yeast	1 tsp.	1½ tsp.	2 tsp.
___			
chopped walnuts	⅓ cup	½ cup	⅔ cup

flour equivalents:	*2 cups*	*3 cups*	*4 cups*
cycle:	*raisin/mix; white, sweet*		
setting:	*light to medium*		

WHEAT RYE NUT BREAD

Use hazelnuts or brazil nuts to give this a distinctive flavor. If using walnuts, try using walnut oil; otherwise, your normal vegetable oil will do.

	Small	Medium	Large
milk/water	3/4 cup	1 1/8 cups	1 1/2 cups
vegetable oil	1 tbs.	1 1/2 tbs.	2 tbs.
honey	1 tbs.	1 1/2 tbs.	2 tbs.
salt	1/3 tsp.	1/2 tsp.	2/3 tsp.
bread flour	3/4 cup	1 1/8 cups	1 1/2 cups
whole wheat flour	3/4 cup	1 1/8 cups	1 1/2 cups
rye flour	1/2 cup	3/4 cup	1 cup
vital gluten, optional	1 1/2 tbs.	2 1/3 tbs.	3 tbs.
yeast	1 1/2 tsp.	2 tsp.	2 1/2 tsp.
————			
chopped nuts	1/4 cup	1/3 cup	1/2 cup

flour equivalents:	*2 cups*	*3 cups*	*4 cups*
cycle:	*raisin/mix; sweet, whole grain*		
setting:	*light to medium*		

WHEAT NUT RAISIN BREAD

This nutty wheat bread is great toasted for breakfast or a snack, with butter and jam or cream cheese and fruit.

	Small	**Medium**	**Large**
water	3/4 cup	1 1/8 cups	1 1/2 cups
walnut oil	2 tbs.	3 tbs.	1/4 cup
molasses	2 tbs.	3 tbs.	1/4 cup
brown sugar	1 tbs.	1 1/3 tbs.	2 tbs.
salt	1/4 tsp.	1/3 tsp.	1/2 tsp.
whole wheat flour	2 cups	3 cups	4 cups
vital gluten, optional	1 to 2 tbs.	1 1/2 to 3 tbs.	2 to 4 tbs.
yeast	1 1/2 tsp.	2 tsp.	2 1/2 tsp.
———			
raisins	1/4 cup	1/3 cup	1/2 cup
chopped walnuts	1/4 cup	1/3 cup	1/2 cup
flour equivalents:	*2 cups*	*3 cups*	*4 cups*
cycle:	*raisin/mix; white, sweet*		
setting:	*light to medium*		

ALMOND POPPY SEED BREAD

A must try! Four stars! This one is worth making for the aroma alone! An outstanding bread for dessert or brunch. If you have problems with "doughy" breads in your machine, see page 6 for tips.

	Small	**Medium**	**Large**
buttermilk	3/4 cup	7/8 cup	1 1/8 cups
butter/margarine	3 tbs.	3 1/2 tbs.	4 tbs.
almond extract	1 tbs.	1 1/3 tbs.	1 1/2 tbs.
brown sugar	1 1/3 tbs.	1 1/2 tbs.	2 tbs.
salt	1/4 tsp.	1/3 tsp.	1/2 tsp.
poppy seeds	1 tbs.	1 1/3 tbs.	1 1/2 tbs.
baking soda	1/4 tsp.	1/3 tsp.	1/2 tsp.
bread flour	2 cups	2 1/2 cups	3 cups
yeast	1 tsp.	1 1/2 tsp.	2 tsp.
chopped almonds	1/3 cup	1/2 cup	2/3 cup
flour equivalents:	*2 cups*	*2 1/2 cups*	*3 cups*
cycle:	raisin/mix; white, sweet		
setting:	light to medium		

ORANGE PISTACHIO BREAD

Wonderful combination of flavors! Serve toasted with pistachio ice cream. A medium-rising loaf of bread.

	Small	Medium	Large
orange juice concentrate	2 tbs.	3 tbs.	¼ cup
orange segments	⅔ cup	1 cup	1⅓ cups
butter/margarine	2 tbs.	3 tbs.	4 tbs.
grated orange peel	¼ tsp.	⅓ tsp.	½ tsp.
salt	⅛ tsp.	⅛+ tsp.	¼ tsp.
whole wheat flour	1 cup	1½ cups	2 cups
bread flour	1 cup	1½ cups	2 cups
yeast	1 tsp.	1½ tsp.	2 tsp.
chopped pistachios	⅓ cup	½ cup	⅔ cup
flour equivalents:	*2 cups*	*3 cups*	*4 cups*
cycle:	*raisin/mix; white, sweet*		
setting:	*light to medium*		

APPLE DATE NUT BREAD

A very aromatic bread with lots of rich flavor. If fresh apples are unavailable, dried apples may be substituted; adjust milk/water if necessary. A great breakfast bread.

	Small	**Medium**	**Large**
milk/water	⅔ cup	1 cup	1⅓ cups
apple juice concentrate	2 tbs.	3 tbs.	¼ cup
applesauce	1 tbs.	1½ tbs.	2 tbs.
salt	¼ tsp.	⅓ tsp.	½ tsp.
cinnamon	¼ tsp.	⅓ tsp.	½ tsp.
whole wheat flour	1 cup	1½ cups	2 cups
bread flour	1 cup	1½ cups	2 cups
yeast	1 tsp.	1½ tsp.	2 tsp.
diced, peeled apple	¼ cup	⅓ cup	½ cup
chopped dates	2 to 3 tbs.	¼ cup	⅓ cup
chopped nuts	¼ cup	⅓ cup	½ cup
flour equivalents:	*2 cups*	*3 cups*	*4 cups*
cycle:	*raisin/mix; white, sweet*		
setting:	*light to medium*		

WHITE CHOCOLATE BREAD

Wow! A wonderful dessert bread. The chips and/or nuts may be adjusted to taste. Coconut or vanilla extract may be substituted for the almond extract if desired.

	Small	Medium	Large
milk	½ cup	5/8 cup	¾ cup
egg	1	1	1½
butter/margarine	2 tbs.	2½ tbs.	3 tbs.
almond extract	1 tsp.	1¼ tsp.	1½ tsp.
salt	¼ tsp.	⅓ tsp.	½ tsp.
sugar	2 tbs.	2½ tbs.	3 tbs.
bread flour	2 cups	2½ cups	3 cups
yeast	1 tsp.	1½ tsp.	2 tsp.
───			
white chocolate chips	¼ cup	⅓ cup	½ cup
chopped nuts	¼ cup	⅓ cup	½ cup

flour equivalents:	*2 cups*	*3 cups*	*4 cups*
cycle:	*raisin/mix; white, sweet*		
setting:	*light*		

POULSBO BREAD

Gaye Levy shares this recipe for Poulsbo bread. This bread, originally developed based on Biblical references to bread, has put Poulsbo, Washington on the map. This is a "must try" — one of the best!

	Small	**Medium**	**Large**
water	3/4 cup	1 1/8 cups	1 1/2 cups
margarine/oil	1 tbs.	1 1/2 tbs.	2 tbs.
molasses	1 1/3 tbs.	2 tbs.	2 2/3 tbs.
sugar	1 1/3 tbs.	2 tbs.	2 2/3 tbs.
salt	1/2 tsp.	3/4 tsp.	1 tsp.
bread flour	1 1/2 cups	2 1/4 cups	3 cups
whole wheat flour	1/4 cup	1/3 cup	1/2 cup
7-grain cereal	1/2 cup	3/4 cup	1 cup
powdered buttermilk	1 tbs.	1 1/2 tbs.	2 tbs.
yeast	1 tsp.	1 1/2 tsp.	2 tsp.
—			
sunflower seeds	1/3 cup	1/2 cup	2/3 cup
flour equivalents:	*2 1/4 cups*	*3 1/3 cups*	*4 1/2 cups*
cycle:	*raisin/mix; white, sweet*		
setting:	*medium*		

PECAN GOUDA BREAD

A devoted fan of bread machines, Wendy Ceracche has been cooking up a storm with her Panasonic for many years now. I know you'll enjoy this. Walnuts may be substituted for the pecans.

	Small	**Medium**	**Large**
water/milk	½ cup	¾ cup	1 cup
margarine/butter	1½ tsp.	2¼ tsp.	1 tbs.
grated Gouda cheese	⅓ cup	½ cup	⅔ cup
sugar	1½ tsp.	2¼ tsp.	1 tbs.
salt	¼ tsp.	⅓ tsp.	½ tsp.
bread flour	1½ cups	2¼ cups	3 cups
yeast	1 tsp.	1½ tsp.	2 tsp.
———			
chopped pecans	¼ cup	⅓ cup	½ cup

flour equivalents:	*1½ cups*	*2¼ cups*	*3 cups*
cycle:	*raisin/mix; white, sweet*		
setting:	*light*		

MEXICAN DATE PECAN BREAD

A wonderful, sweet bread. Serve with amaretto coffee and whipped cream for a real treat. It also makes great toast or French toast.

	Small	**Medium**	**Large**
milk	⅔ cup	¾ cup	1 cup
butter/margarine	1 tbs.	1½ tbs.	2 tbs.
salt	¼ tsp.	⅓ tsp.	½ tsp.
sugar (white)	2 tbs.	2½ tbs.	3 tbs.
cinnamon	½ tsp.	⅔ tsp.	¾ tsp.
nutmeg	⅛ tsp.	⅛+ tsp.	¼ tsp.
bread flour	2 cups	2½ cups	3 cups
yeast	1 tsp.	1½ tsp.	2 tsp.
―――			
chopped dates	⅓ cup	⅓+ cup	½ cup
chopped pecans	¼ cup	⅓ cup	⅓+ cup

flour equivalents: *2 cups*   *2½ cups*   *3 cups*
cycle: *raisin/mix; white, sweet*
setting: *light to medium*

BLACK WALNUT BREAD

Black walnuts are richer and more flavorful than the English walnuts. This bread takes full advantage of the distinctive black walnut taste.

	Small	**Medium**	**Large**
buttermilk	¾ cup	scant 1 cup	1⅛ cups
walnut oil	1 tbs.	1⅓ tbs.	1½ tbs.
honey	2 tbs.	2½ tbs.	3 tbs.
salt	¼ tsp.	⅓ tsp.	½ tsp.
baking soda	¼ tsp.	¼+ tsp.	⅓ tsp.
coconut flakes	¼ cup	¼+ cup	⅓ cup
oats	½ cup	⅝ cup	¾ cup
bread flour	1½ cups	1⅞ cups	2¼ cups
yeast	1 tsp.	1½ tsp.	2 tsp.
chopped black walnuts	⅓ cup	½ cup	⅔ cup
flour equivalents:	*2 cups*	*3 cups*	*4 cups*
cycle:	*raisin/mix; white, sweet*		
setting:	*light*		

MACADAMIA NUT BREAD

This is a "must try" — a delicious sweet bread which is great toasted for breakfast or brunch or served with dessert.

	Small	**Medium**	**Large**
buttermilk	3/4 cup	1 1/8 cups	1 1/2 cups
butter/margarine	1 tbs.	1 1/2 tbs.	2 tbs.
maple/brown sugar	2 tbs.	3 tbs.	1/4 cup
salt	1/3 tsp.	1/2 tsp.	2/3 tsp.
baking soda	1/4 tsp.	1/3 tsp.	1/2 tsp.
ground ginger	1/4 tsp.	1/3 tsp.	1/2 tsp.
oats	1/2 cup	3/4 cup	1 cup
coconut flakes	1/4 cup	1/3 cup	1/2 cup
bread flour	1 1/2 cups	2 1/4 cups	3 cups
yeast	1 tsp.	1 1/2 tsp.	2 tsp.
——			
chopped macadamias	1/3 cup	1/2 cup	2/3 cup
flour equivalents:	*2+ cups*	*3+ cups*	*4+ cups*
cycle:	*raisin/mix; white, sweet*		
setting:	*light to medium*		

SUNFLOWER HONEY BREAD

Heather Smith of Southern California adapted this recipe and receives rave reviews. The sunflower seeds, in this case, replace some of the flour. If you have sunflower oil, use it as the vegetable oil for extra flavoring. The salt may be halved if desired.

	Small	**Medium**	**Large**
milk or water	⅔ cup	1 cups	1⅓ cups
vegetable oil	1⅓ tbs.	2 tbs.	2⅔ tbs.
honey	1⅓ tbs.	2 tbs.	2⅔ tbs.
salt	⅔ tsp.	1 tsp.	1⅓ tsp.
whole wheat flour	½ cup	¾ cup	1 cup
sunflower seeds	¼ cup	⅓ cup	½ cup
bread flour	1 cup	1½ cups	2 cups
yeast	1 tsp.	1½ tsp.	2 tsp.

flour equivalents:	*1¾ cups*	*2½+ cups*	*3½ cups*
cycle:	*white, sweet; timer with water*		
setting:	*medium*		

CHERRY NUT BREAD

*This colorful loaf really picks up the flavor of the cherries. Dried cherries are available through gourmet shops or mail order catalogs (see **Sources**, page 183).*

	Small	**Medium**	**Large**
milk	¾ cup	1⅛ cups	1½ cups
vegetable oil	1 tbs.	1½ tbs.	2 tbs.
honey	2 tbs.	3 tbs.	¼ cup
salt	⅓ tsp.	½ tsp.	⅔ tsp.
oats	½ cup	¾ cup	1 cup
bread flour	1½ cups	2¼ cups	3 cups
yeast	1 tsp.	1½ tsp.	2 tsp.
——			
dried cherries	⅓ cup	½ cup	⅔ cup
chopped nuts	¼ cup	⅓ cup	½ cup

flour equivalents:	*2 cups*	*3 cups*	*4 cups*
cycle:	*raisin/mix; white, sweet*		
setting:	*light to medium*		

ORANGE NUT BREAD

This is one of our favorite combinations. Use your favorite nuts — I like Brazil nuts with this bread. Of course, the bread is also delicious without the nuts too! For variation, substitute raisins or dried cranberries for the nuts.

	Small	**Medium**	**Large**
buttermilk	3/4 cup	1 1/8 cups	1 1/2 cups
orange juice concentrate	2 tbs.	3 tbs.	4 tbs.
honey	2 tbs.	3 tbs.	4 tbs.
salt	1/3 tsp.	1/2 tsp.	2/3 tsp.
baking soda	1/4 to 1/2 tsp.	1/3 to 3/4 tsp.	1/2 to 1 tsp.
oats	1/2 cup	3/4 cup	1 cup
bread flour	1 1/2 cups	2 1/4 cups	3 cups
yeast	1 tsp.	1 1/2 tsp.	2 tsp.
———			
chopped nuts	1/3 cup	1/2 cup	2/3 cup
flour equivalents:	*2 cups*	*3 cups*	*4 cups*
cycle:	*raisin/mix; sweet; no timer*		
setting:	*light*		

WHITE CHOCOLATE MACADAMIA BREAD

The result of many requests, this has become a favorite in our house! If macadamia nuts are unavailable or too expensive, almonds may also be used.

	Small	**Medium**	**Large**
milk	½ cup	⅔ cup	¾ cup
white chocolate chips	¼ cup	⅓ cup	½ cup
egg	1	1½	1½
butter/margarine	2 tbs.	2½ tbs.	3 tbs.
almond extract	1 tsp.	1¼ tsp.	1½ tsp.
sugar	2 tbs.	2½ tbs.	3 tbs.
salt	¼ tsp.	⅓ tsp.	½ tsp.
bread flour	2 cups	2½ cups	3 cups
yeast	1 tsp.	1½ tsp.	2 tsp.
———			
chopped macadamias	⅓ cup	½ cup	⅔ cup

flour equivalents:	*2 cups*	*2½ cups*	*3 cups*
cycle:	*raisin/mix, white, sweet; no timer*		
setting:	*light*		

CREAMED CINNAMON RAISIN NUT BREAD

*A wonderful raisin nut bread. Top with powdered sugar or **Confectioners' Sugar Glaze**, page 168 for a major hit in your house. If watching calories, evaporated skim milk may be substituted for the whipping cream.*

	Small	Medium	Large
whipping cream	¾ cup	1⅛ cups	1½ cups
butter/margarine	2 tbs.	3 tbs.	4 tbs.
egg	1	1½	2
sugar	2 tsp.	1 tbs.	1⅓ tbs.
cinnamon	½ tsp.	¾ tsp.	1 tsp.
salt	¼ tsp.	⅓ tsp.	½ tsp.
whole wheat flour	1 cup	1½ cups	2 cups
bread flour	1 cup	1½ cups	2 cups
yeast	1 tsp.	1½ tsp.	2 tsp.
raisins	¼ cup	⅓ cup	½ cup
nuts, chopped	3 tbs.	4½ tbs.	6 tbs.
flour equivalents:	*2 cups*	*3 cups*	*4 cups*
cycle:	*raisin/mix; white, sweet*		
setting:	*light to medium*		

COCONUT CHOCOLATE BREAD

This is absolutely incredible. Chips may become ground up depending on which machine you have, but either way it is equally delicious. Eat it as a dessert, snack or for breakfast or brunch. You can substitute walnuts or pecans for macadamias.

	Small	**Medium**	**Large**
water	2/3 cup	7/8 cup	1 cup
vegetable oil	2 tsp.	1 tbs.	1 1/3 tbs.
coconut extract	2 tsp.	1 tbs.	1 1/3 tbs.
salt	1/8 to 1/4 tsp.	1/8+ to 1/3 tsp.	1/4 to 1/2 tsp.
coconut flakes	1/3 cup	1/2 cup	2/3 cup
bread flour	2 cups	2 1/2 cups	3 cups
yeast	1 tsp.	1 1/2 tsp.	2 tsp.
───			
chocolate chips	1/3 cup	1/2 cup	2/3 cup
chopped macadamias	1/4 cup	1/3 cup	1/2 cup
flour equivalents:	*2 cups*	*2 1/2 cups*	*3 cups*
cycle:	*raisin/mix; white, sweet*		
setting:	*light*		

ROLLS AND COFFEE CAKES

One of the joys of owning a bread machine is the ability to make delicious yeasted coffee cakes or rolls with relatively little effort. The machine does the initial kneading (the hardest part) and allows the dough to rise for the first time. Once the dough is removed from the machine, it can be filled and shaped and allowed to rise a second time prior to baking in a conventional oven.

This chapter has several sweet and non-sweet dough recipes which may be used with fillings found on pages 178-182. You can pick and choose both the dough and the filling you want and follow any of the suggested shaping and baking guidelines to achieve your desired coffee cake or rolls. All dough recipes are made using the basic dough cycle. Various washes, which are brushed on the loaves/rolls just prior to baking, are also provided as suggestions. I find that I do not like allowing the dough to knead or rise a second time in the machine (DAK or Welbilt ABM 100) and recommend that you turn the machine off after approximately 1 hour and use the dough then.

If the dough is too sticky to roll, simply add flour a little at a time until it may be handled. Don't overflour. Remember that ovens vary and that cooking times may also vary. As with any baking, keep an eye on the oven to avoid burning.

SHAPING AND BAKING GUIDELINES

CRESCENTS
Remove dough from machine and roll into 1 or 2 circles. Brush with melted butter or a very thin filling and cut circles into 8 pieces. Roll each piece, starting from thick end, into the center, forming a crescent shape. Brush top with any remaining butter. Place on a greased baking sheet, cover and let rise for approximately 30 minutes. Bake in a preheated 325° oven for about 20 minutes or until golden brown.

COFFEE CAKE ROLLS

Punch down dough and divide in half if making the medium or large recipe. On a lightly floured surface, roll the dough into a rectangle and spread with filling ingredients. Jelly-roll starting at the wide end, pinch the ends and cut into rolls. Place in 1 or 2 greased 9-inch round or square cake pans. An alternative is to place each roll in a greased muffin tin. Cover and let rise in a warm, draft-free location approximately 1 hour. Brush with wash if desired and bake in a preheated 350° oven for 20 to 25 minutes.

MONKEY BREAD

Remove dough from machine and separate into as many 1- to 1½-inch balls as you can. Roll the balls in melted butter and then a coating such as finely chopped nuts, grated Parmesan cheese or even herbs. Place the balls into a greased loaf pan, tube pan or holiday-shaped pan (such as a Christmas tree), cover and let rise for approximately 1 hour. Brush with wash if desired, and bake in a preheated 350° oven for 30 to 40 minutes or until golden brown.

WREATH

Remove the dough from the machine. Roll the dough into 1 or 2 rectangles and spread filling (if applicable) on top. Roll in a jelly-roll fashion starting at the wide end. Form this into 1 or 2 circles, pinching the seam closed. With scissors, cut at 2/3- to 1-inch intervals and turn cut sections up. Place on a greased baking sheet, cover and let rise for approximately 45 minutes. Brush with wash if desired and bake in a preheated 350° oven for 30 to 40 minutes or until golden brown.

JELLY ROLL

Remove dough from machine and roll into 1 or 2 rectangles. Spread filling evenly on top. Roll in a jelly-roll fashion starting at the wide end. Pinch seams closed. Place seam side down on a greased baking sheet or in a greased bread pan (or 2), cover and let rise about 30 to 45 minutes. Brush with wash if desired and bake in a preheated 350° oven for approximately 30 to 40 minutes or until golden and it sounds hollow when tapped.

STROMBOLI ROLL

Remove dough from machine and roll into 1 or 2 rectangles. Spread filling mixture on top of middle third of rectangle and fold each side over top of filling so that it is encased. Pinch ends closed and place fold side down on a well greased baking sheet. Brush top with wash if desired. Bake in a preheated 350° for 20 to 30 minutes or until golden brown.

PIZZA

One trick to a thin, crispy pizza crust is rolling the dough as thin as you can. Trim it to fit your pan. Using a pizza stone or a pizza pan with holes in the bottom will result in a crispier crust. If desired, the leftover dough may be used to make bread sticks.

Remove the dough from the machine and roll into a circle or rectangle depending on what pan you are using. Place on your greased or cornmeal covered pan and top as desired. Do not let rise a second time. There are two thoughts on baking pizza. The first is to put it into a cold oven and turn the oven on to 500°; bake until golden brown and cheese is melted. The second is to bake on a pizza stone or the bottom (not the rack) of a preheated 500° oven until the pizza is golden brown and cheese is melted. This could range from 10 to 30 minutes depending on which method you use.

A tip: I keep pizza dough in a plastic bag in the refrigerator and use as needed. It makes for a quick throw-together meal with spaghetti sauce or pizza sauce and grated cheese. The dough lasts for several days this way. I just remove it and roll it out while it is still cold.

ENGLISH MUFFINS

Remove dough from machine upon its completion. Roll or press the dough so that it is approximately ⅓- to ½-inch thick on a greased and cornmeal-covered baking sheet. Cut into circles of approximately 3 inches in diameter, using a biscuit or cookie cutter, removing excess dough. (A tuna fish size can would be perfect as well!). Leave the dough as is, cover and place in a warm, draft-free location for approximately 1 to 2 hours. Sprinkle with more cornmeal if desired and then cook the muffins in a lightly greased frying pan or griddle for 5 to 7 minutes on each side until both sides are golden brown. Be sure not to burn. Allow to cool on a wire rack.

FRENCH BREAD

Remove dough from machine and roll on a cornmeal-covered surface into one or two rectangles. Jelly-roll the rectangles, starting at a wide end; pinch ends closed. Place the loaves on a greased baking sheet which has been sprinkled with cornmeal to prevent sticking. (I use a pizza pan with holes in the bottom which makes the crust crustier.) Cover and let rise in a warm location for 40 to 50 minutes.

Slash the dough 5 or 6 times with a sharp knife or razor blade and brush with cold water. Bake in a preheated 400° oven for 15 minutes and then lower temperature to 350° and bake for 5 to 10 minutes or until golden brown and bread sounds hollow when tapped.

COCONUT SWEET DOUGH

*Try this with the following fillings: **Orange Coconut**, page 179, and **Orange**, page 178.*

	Small	Medium	Large
buttermilk	⅔ cup	1 cup	1⅓ cups
butter/margarine	1 tbs.	1½ tbs.	2 tbs.
egg	1	1½	2
sugar	2 tbs.	3 tbs.	¼ cup
baking soda	¼ tsp.	⅓ tsp.	½ tsp.
salt	⅓ tsp.	½ tsp.	⅔ tsp.
coconut flakes	½ cup	¾ cup	1 cup
bread flour	2 cups	3 cups	4 cups
yeast	1 tsp.	1½ tsp.	2 tsp.
wash with:			
melted butter	1 tbs.	1½ tbs.	2 tbs.
coconut extract	¼ tsp.	⅓ tsp.	½ tsp.
flour equivalents:	*2½ cups*	*3¾ cups*	*5 cups*

ORANGE SWEET DOUGH

*Try this dough with **Orange Coconut** filling, page 179, **Praline Rolling Filling**, page 179 or **Orange Filling**, page 178.*

	Small	Medium	Large
milk	½ cup	¾ cup	1 cup
butter/margarine	2 tbs.	3 tbs.	4 tbs.
orange extract	½ tsp.	¾ tsp.	1 tsp.
egg	1	1½	2
orange peel	⅛ tsp.	⅛+ tsp.	¼ tsp.
sugar	2 tbs.	3 tbs.	4 tbs.
salt	¼ tsp.	⅓ tsp.	½ tsp.
bread flour	2 cups	3 cups	4 cups
yeast	1 tsp.	1½ tsp.	2 tsp.
flour equivalents:	*2½ cups*	*3¾ cups*	*5 cups*

SWEET YEAST DOUGH

Sandra Farace says she uses this recipe for everything from a stollen to cinnamon or caramel rolls. Sandra has been baking yeast breads for 23 years and does not use a bread machine. I have adapted her recipe for the machines.

	Small	Medium	Large
heavy cream	½ cup	¾ cup	1 cup
evaporated milk	2 tbs.	3 tbs.	¼ cup
egg yolks	1	2	3
butter/margarine	4 tbs.	6 tbs.	8 tbs.
sugar (white)	2 tbs.	3 tbs.	¼ cup
salt	½ tsp.	¾ tsp.	1 tsp.
cinnamon	½ tsp.	¾ tsp.	1 tsp.
nutmeg	½ tsp.	¾ tsp.	1 tsp.
bread flour	1⅔ cups	2½ cups	3⅓ cups
yeast	1 tsp.	1½ tsp.	2 tsp.
flour equivalents:	*1⅔ cups*	*2½ cups*	*3⅓ cups*

BUTTERMILK DOUGH

A wonderful dough which goes nicely with everything from pizza to sweets.

	Small	**Medium**	**Large**
buttermilk	3/4 cup	1 1/8 cups	1 1/2 cups
white/brown sugar	1 tsp.	1 1/2 tsp.	2 tsp.
salt	1/4 tsp.	1/3 tsp.	1/2 tsp.
baking soda	1/4 tsp.	1/3 tsp.	1/2 tsp.
bread flour	2 cups	3 cups	4 cups
yeast	1 tsp.	1 1/2 tsp.	2 tsp.

LEMON DOUGH

*Use **Spinach Filling**, page 181, for a delicious meal.*

water	2/3 cup	1 cup	1 1/3 cups
lemon juice	1 1/2 tsp.	2 1/4 tsp.	1 tbs.
olive oil	1 1/2 tsp.	2 1/4 tsp.	1 tbs.
sugar	1 tsp.	1 1/2 tsp.	2 tsp.
salt	dash	1/8 tsp.	1/8+ tsp.
bread flour	2 cups	3 cups	4 cups
yeast	1 tsp.	1 1/2 tsp.	2 tsp.
flour equivalents (each recipe):	*2 cups*	*3 cups*	*4 cups*

APPLE DOUGH

*Fill this with **Sausage Filling**, page 181, for an absolutely unbeatable combination. You must try this one. Watch the dough about 5 minutes into the kneading. If it looks too dry (balls or crumbly) add apple juice 1 tbs. at a time until one nice round ball is formed.*

	Small	Medium	Large
apple juice	2/3 cup	1 cup	1 1/3 cups
olive oil	1 tbs.	1 1/2 tbs.	2 tbs.
honey	1 tbs.	1 1/2 tbs.	2 tbs.
salt	1/4 tsp.	1/3 tsp.	1/2 tsp.
rosemary	1/2 tsp.	3/4 tsp.	1 tsp.
whole wheat flour	1 cup	1 1/2 cups	2 cups
bread flour	1 cup	1 1/2 cups	2 cups
yeast	1 tsp.	1 1/2 tsp.	2 tsp.
flour equivalents:	*2 cups*	*3 cups*	*4 cups*

SPINACH DOUGH

Cook and drain the spinach and use all purpose or bread flour. Suggested fillings: spinach or cheese. This dough may also be used for a different and unique pizza dough with the cheese filling used as a topping instead of the more familiar tomato topping.

	Small	Medium	Large
water	½ cup	¾ cup	1 cup
spinach	½ cup	¾ cup	1 cup
lemon juice	2 tsp.	1 tbs.	1⅓ tbs.
olive oil	2 tsp.	1 tbs.	1⅓ tbs.
sugar	1 tsp.	1½ tsp.	2 tsp.
salt	¼ tsp.	⅓ tsp.	½ tsp.
flour	2 cups	3 cups	4 cups
yeast	1 tsp.	1½ tsp.	2 tsp.
flour equivalents:	*2 cups*	*3 cups*	*4 cups*

SOURDOUGH DOUGH

Say this ten times really fast! This a basic dough which goes well with anything and everything.

	Small	Medium	Large
starter	½ cup	¾ cup	1 cup
milk/water	½ cup	¾ cup	1 cup
olive oil	2 tsp.	1 tbs.	1⅓ tbs.
sugar	⅔ tsp.	1 tsp.	1⅓ tsp.
salt	¼ tsp.	⅓ tsp.	½ tsp.
bread flour	2 cups	3 cups	4 cups
yeast	1 tsp.	1½ tsp.	2 tsp.
flour equivalents:	*2 cups*	*3 cups*	*4 cups*

PIZZA DOUGH

This is our current pizza dough recipe — we are always looking for new ones. Whole wheat or any other flour may be substituted for half or all of the bread flour. If using flours such as amaranth or quinoa for their high nutritional content, start off using only a small portion (1/4-1/3 total amount) and adjust to taste. Follow directions for pizza, page 146, or fill following directions for stromboli or jelly roll.

	Small	**Medium**	**Large**
water	2/3 cup	1 cup	1 1/3 cups
olive oil	2 tbs.	3 tbs.	1/4 cup
salt	1/4 tsp.	1/3 tsp.	1/2 tsp.
sugar	1/2 tsp.	3/4 tsp.	1 tsp.
bread flour	2 cups	3 cups	4 cups
yeast	1 tsp.	1 1/2 tsp.	2 tsp.
flour equivalents:	*2 cups*	*3 cups*	*4 cups*

FRUCTOSE CINNAMON ROLLS

Andrea Hebert-Donatelli adapts recipes to use fructose instead of sugar. This is one of her family's favorite recipes. Follow directions for coffee cake rolls, page 144. Pour cream (room temperature) on top before baking to glaze.

	Small	**Medium**	**Large**
milk	½ cup	¾ cup	1 cup
egg(s)	1	1½	2
butter/margarine	2 tbs.	3 tbs.	4 tbs.
salt	⅓ tsp.	½ tsp.	¾ tsp.
fructose	2½ tbs.	¼ cup	⅓ cup
all purpose flour	1¾ cups	2⅔ cups	3½ cups
yeast	1 tsp.	1½ tsp.	2 tsp.
filling			
butter, softened	2 tbs.	3 tbs.	4 tbs.
raisins	¼ cup	⅓ cup	½ cup
fructose	2 tbs.	3 tbs.	¼ cup
cinnamon	1 tsp.	1½ tsp.	2 tsp.
whipping cream	½, cup	¾ cup	1 cup
flour equivalents:	*1¾ cups*	*2⅔ cups*	*3½ cups*

BUTTER CRESCENTS

This sweet, buttery dough may also be used as a basis for any coffee cake or sweet rolls. This recipe may also be baked in your bread machine for a delicious, sweet bread. Be sure to use the sweet cycle if applicable and not to overfill the size of your machine as it's a high-rising loaf. Follow directions for crescents, page 143.

	Small	Medium	Large
milk	½ cup	¾ cup	1 cup
butter	4 tbs.	6 tbs.	8 tbs.
egg	1	1½	2
sugar	¼ cup	⅓ cup	½ cup
salt	¼ tsp.	⅓ tsp.	½ tsp.
all purpose flour	2 cups	3 cups	4 cups
yeast	1 tsp.	1½ tsp.	2 tsp.
filling			
melted butter	1 tbs.	1½ tbs.	2 tbs.
flour equivalents:	*2 cups*	*3 cups*	*4 cups*

CHOCOLATE CREAM CHEESE ROLLS

A tester of recipes, Debbie Nicholson developed this recipe to cover two of her favorite foods, cream cheese and chocolate. Follow directions for jelly roll or stromboli, page 145. Beat the cream cheese and powdered sugar together; spread this on top of dough and layer chocolate chips and nuts on top of that.

	Small	Medium	Large
milk	½ cup	¾ cup	1 cup
cream cheese	¼ cup	⅜ cup	½ cup
sugar	2 tbs.	3 tbs.	¼ cup
eggs	1	1½	2
salt	⅓ tsp.	½ tsp.	⅔ tsp.
bread flour	2 cups	3 cups	4 cups
yeast	1 tsp.	1½ tsp.	2 tsp.

filling

	Small	Medium	Large
cream cheese	4 oz.	6 oz.	8 oz.
powdered sugar	½ cup	¾ cup	1 cup
chocolate chips	¼ cup	⅓ cup	½ cup
chopped nuts, optional	½ cup	¾ cup	1 cup
flour equivalents:	*2 cups*	*3 cups*	*4 cups*

TRADITIONAL FRENCH BREAD

Combine the ease of making the dough in the machine with the traditional French bread shape for a true winner. For an extra crispy loaf, put a pan of water on the bottom rack of the oven during baking. Another trick is to use a ceramic or clay pizza or baking stone for an extra crispy crust.

	Small	Medium	Large
water	3/4 cup	1 cup	1 1/8 cups
sugar	1/3 tsp.	1/2 tsp.	2/3 tsp.
salt	2/3 tsp.	1 tsp.	1 1/3 tsp.
bread flour	2/3 cup	3/4 cup	1 cup
cake flour	1 1/3 cups	1 1/2 cups	2 cups
yeast	1 1/2 tsp.	2 tsp.	2 1/2 tsp.
cornmeal for shaping			

Allow the dough to rise in the machine for at least 1 1/2 hours - even if the machine has stopped. Punch down the dough while it is still in the pan in the machine and allow it to rise in the turned off but still warm machine or other warm, draft-free location for 30 to 40 minutes. See page 147 for shaping and baking guidelines.

flour equivalents:	*2 cups*	*2 1/4 cups*	*3 cups*

ENGLISH MUFFINS I

Perhaps the only purchased bread which I have actually missed (but still refuse to buy) are English muffins. After years of thinking it looked too difficult to figure out, I finally attempted it — to rave reviews. These have now become an easy staple in our household. If farina is not on hand, cream of wheat may be used instead. See **Shaping and Baking Guidelines**, page 146.

	Small (10)	Medium (15)	Large (20)
milk	¾ cup	1⅛ cups	1½ cups
corn syrup	1 tbs.	1½ tbs.	2 tbs.
salt	⅓ tsp.	½ tsp.	⅔ tsp.
farina	¼ cup	⅓ cup	½ cup
all purpose flour	1¾ cups	2⅔ cups	3½ cups
yeast	1 tsp.	1½ tsp.	2 tsp.
flour equivalents:	*2 cups*	*3 cups*	*4 cups*

ENGLISH MUFFINS II

I really like playing around with this recipe, using orange juice with a little orange peel, apple juice with raisins added, using half whole wheat. The variations are unlimited! For instance, use buttermilk in place of the milk or water and add baking soda, 1/4 tsp. 1/3 tsp. 1/2 tsp. See **Shaping and Baking Guidelines**, *page 146.*

	Small (10)	Medium (15)	Large (20)
milk or water	3/4 cup	1 1/8 cups	1 1/2 cups
butter/margarine	1 tbs.	1 1/2 tbs.	2 tbs.
sugar	2 tsp.	1 tbs.	1 1/3 tbs.
salt	1/3 tsp.	1/2 tsp.	2/3 tsp.
all purpose flour	2 cups	3 cups	4 cups
yeast	1 tsp.	1 1/2 tsp.	2 tsp.
flour equivalents	*2 cups*	*3 cups*	*4 cups*

EGG PASTA DOUGH

Andy Hebert-Donatelli became frustrated when her husband no longer had the time to make their pasta dough. Not liking the way it turned out in her Kitchen Aid, she decided to try the bread machine. Low and behold, she says it's perfect.

Servings:	3-4	5-6	7-8
eggs	3	4	6
all purpose flour	2¼ cups	3 cups	4½ cups

Put flour in the pan and crack the eggs into the center of the flour. Start the machine and check to make sure it isn't working too hard. If so, add a tablespoon of cold water at a time until it is kneading without trouble. (She usually does not have to do this.) Remove the dough as soon as the kneading has stopped. Check the dough before rolling by inserting a finger into the center; if it comes out almost dry, then it is ready to use. Take small pieces of dough at a time and roll it to the thickness of the noodle you want and slice it lengthwise. Flour the noodles and set them aside. You can hang them on a drying rack, but Andy uses hers right away. To cook fresh noodles, bring to a boil ⅔ large pan of salted water. Add pasta and bring water back to a boil, cooking uncovered for 5 to 20 seconds after the water returns to a boil. DO NOT OVERCOOK PASTA! If your pasta is more than a day old, it requires longer cooking.

NAN

A flat bread from India which makes a great alternative to bagels. While the traditional Nan has onions, try substituting lemon or orange peel, anise or fennel.

	2	**3**	**4**
water	¼ cup	⅓ cup	½ cup
yogurt (plain)	½ cup	¾ cup	1 cup
butter	1½ tbs.	2 tbs.	3 tbs.
sugar	1 tsp.	1½ tsp.	2 tsp.
salt	⅛ tsp.	⅛+ tsp.	¼ tsp.
all purpose flour	2 cups	3 cups	4 cups
yeast	1 tsp.	1½ tsp.	2 tsp.
topping			
melted butter	1 tbs.	1½ tbs.	2 tbs.
onion, finely diced	1 to 2 tbs.	1½ to 3 tbs.	3 to 4 tbs.

Upon removing dough from machine, divide into the appropriate number of pieces. Roll each piece into a small 7- to 8-inch circle and place on a greased pizza or baking pan. Brush tops with melted butter; press onion slivers into the dough. Bake in a preheated 500° oven for 10 to 15 minutes until puffy and brown.

flour equivalents: *2 cups*   *3 cups*   *4 cups*

TOPPINGS AND FILLINGS

Toppings may be served along with individual slices of bread, much as you would butter and/or jelly or jam.

Glazes are used as a type of frosting, covering an entire loaf of bread. Cover the loaf while it is still warm and allow the glaze to dry.

Washes are brushed onto the loaves/rolls just prior to baking as a finishing touch. Any of the following may be used. If using a wash, be sure to cover the entire top — don't miss a section or it will bake a different color.

Butter wash - Use melted butter with or without an extract mixed in. I like using extract (1/4 tsp. of extract for every 1 tbs. of butter) to pick up the flavor of the bread. For example, if the bread has almonds in it, I'll add 1/4 tsp. of almond extract to 1 tbs. of melted butter.

Egg wash - Many people use a beaten egg, either whole or egg white only.

Cold water wash - A few tablespoons of cold water are effective in achieving a crispy crust. A pinch of salt may be added if desired although I do not feel it necessary.

Seeds and nuts with washes - Once a wash has been used (usually the egg or water), sprinkle a tablespoon or two of any of the following seeds or very finely ground nuts evenly over the top as an additional treat. Try anise, caraway, celery, coriander, dill, fennel, poppy or sesame seeds; or even a coarse sea salt may also be used. Consider the flavor of the bread and make sure that the tastes will blend.

Using seeds and nuts with washes for loaves baked in the machine is possible too! Just open the lid towards the end of the second rising and sprinkle the desired seeds/nuts on top of the loaf. Try not to spill them down the side of the pan.

Fillings are used for coffee cake breads. Select your filling to match the dough. For example, make coffee cake rolls with a sweet dough and corresponding sweet filling. Recipes created specifically for fillings are provided in three amounts which correspond to the doughs. Recipes for toppings which may also be used for fillings may be easily doubled if desired. Spread just enough on the dough so the dough is covered; keep any remaining topping on hand to serve later.

Follow directions for filling coffee cakes and breads found on pages 143-145. For sweet coffee cake or dessert type breads, I prefer using crescents, coffee cake rolls, monkey bread, wreath or jelly roll formations. For sandwich rolls or meals, I prefer using the directions for jelly rolls, stromboli or pizza.

In addition to the few fillings listed here, try your favorite sandwich fillings or leftovers. For 175 wonderful and exciting filling ideas, see my book, **THE SANDWICH MAKER COOKBOOK**.

Unless otherwise stated, all filling ingredients are mixed together using a mixer, blender or food processor.

ORANGE GLAZE

This may be drizzled on top of any orange bread or rolls while still hot. Allow to cool and then serve. Makes ½ cup.

½ cup confectioners' sugar

1 tbs. butter, melted

1 tbs. orange juice

ORANGE HONEY SYRUP

The thinner (1 tsp. cornstarch) version of this may be used as a glaze and the thicker version (2 tsp. cornstarch) may be served as a topping or filling. Mix ingredients together in a saucepan and bring to a boil, stirring constantly. Heat until thickened. Makes 1¼ cups.

⅔ cup orange juice

½ cup honey

½ tsp orange peel

1 to 2 tsp. cornstarch

CONFECTIONERS' SUGAR GLAZE

Mix ingredients until desired consistency is obtained. Pour over bread while it is still hot. Other extracts such as almond or coconut may be used in place of the vanilla if desired. Makes approximately 1 cup.

1 cup confectioners' sugar (approximately)
1 tbs. milk
1/4 tsp. vanilla extract

CHOCOLATE SAUCE

Wonderful is the best word to describe this! Use as a glaze or as a thin topping. Heat cream and honey until warm — do not boil. Add chocolate chips and stir until chocolate has melted. Pour over a sweet bread and allow to cool or eat warm. Makes approximately 3/4 cup. For variety, add 2 tbs. coconut flakes — truly decadent!

1/3 cup heavy cream
2 tbs. honey
1/2 cup semisweet chocolate chips

HERB BUTTER

Use this as either a topping or a filling for swirled dinner rolls (follow directions for coffee cake rolls). Pair with a pizza, sourdough or buttermilk dough. Makes approximately ½ cup.

4 tbs. softened butter or ¼ cup yogurt cheese or cream cheese
½ tsp. dried chives or 1½ tsp. diced green onion (scallion)
½ tsp. dried oregano or basil (1½ tsp. fresh, crumbled)
½ tsp. dried parsley (1½ tsp. fresh, crumbled)

ORANGE HONEY BUTTER

This decadent butter or cheese may be used as either a topping or a filling for a coffee cake. If using as a filling, glaze the top with orange glaze and sprinkle with some nuts. Use a sweet dough. Makes approximately ¾ cup.

½ cup softened butter, yogurt
   cheese or cream cheese
¼ cup honey

2 tbs. orange juice concentrate
¼ tsp. grated orange peel

GINGERED PEACH SPREAD

Chop ginger in food processor (steel blade) or blender until finely crumbled and add butter/margarine until both are creamed together. Gently mix in preserves. Orange marmalade may be substituted for the preserves if desired. May be chilled and used as a topping or could be used as a filling with a basic sweet yeast or buttermilk dough. Makes approximately ½ cup.

4 tbs. butter/margarine

½ to ¾ tsp. crystallized ginger

¼ cup peach preserves

STRAWBERRY TOPPING

This is absolutely delicious. A sweet, decadent topping to serve with toast for breakfast or brunch. This also makes a great filling with a sweet dough. Cream the softened cream cheese, add the sugar until well mixed in and then fold in the strawberries. Serve chilled or warmed from the microwave. Makes approximately ½ cup.

4 oz. cream cheese, softened

½ cup confectioners' sugar

1 tbs. pureed strawberries or
   strawberry preserves

SPICY BUTTER

Wonderful served with any apple or raisin bread. Combine ingredients with mixer or in food processor until well blended. Serve room temperature. Makes approximately 1/4 cup.

4 tbs. butter, softened   1/2 tsp. pumpkin pie spice
1 tsp. honey

CRANBERRY BUTTER

Pure delight for a festive fall treat. Mix butter and confectioners' sugar in food processor (steel blade) or blender until well blended. Add orange peel and cranberries and process/blend until just mixed in. Shape with individual butter molds, cookie cutters or into a ball. May be served chilled or at room temperature. Butter may be refrigerated for several days. Makes approximately 1/2 cup.

1 stick unsalted butter, softened   1/8 tsp. orange peel
2 tbs. confectioners' sugar   3 tbs. chopped fresh cranberries

ORANGE TOPPING

Serve with any raisin or cranberry bread. Delicious. Cream the softened cream cheese and mix in the remaining ingredients. Serve chilled or warmed from the microwave. Makes approximately ½ cup.

4 oz. cream cheese, softened
½ cup confectioners' sugar

4 to 5 mandarin orange segments
⅛ tsp. orange peel

SAUTÉED APPLE TOPPING

*Absolutely superb — serve with any oatmeal, raisin or apple bread. Melt butter/margarine in pan over low heat. Add apple and cinnamon and sauté until crisp bordering on tender. Makes approximately ¾ cup. For **Maple Apple Topping,** omit cinnamon and use 2 tbs. maple syrup.*

1 medium apple, peeled and thinly
  sliced or diced

¼ tsp. cinnamon
1 tbs. butter/margarine

BUTTERED PRESERVES

A wonderful, easy topping. No additional syrups or butters required. Serve softened at room temperature. Cream butter and add preserves until well blended. I use the food processor with a steel blade, a mixer or blender could also be used. Makes approximately ½ cup.

4 tbs. unsalted butter, softened
¼ cup favorite preserve (strawberry, apricot, peach, etc.)

FRUITED HONEY

Creamy honey with your favorite fruits makes for a terrific topping to bread! Suggested concentrates: orange, apple, grape, strawberry, blueberry, blackberry, raspberry. Keep refrigerated. Makes approximately ¼ cup.

¼ cup honey
1 tbs. fruit juice concentrate

SPICED HONEY

A delectable topping for toast of all kinds. Mix ingredients together and serve at room temperature. Keep refrigerated. Makes ¼ cup.

¼ cup honey
½ tsp. cinnamon
⅛ tsp. nutmeg
⅛ tsp. cloves

PEANUT BUTTER AND HONEY

Children will ask for toast just to eat this topping! May also be served with jelly in a sandwich, or add mashed banana. Mix together and serve at room temperature. Keep refrigerated. Makes approximately ⅓ cup.

¼ cup honey
2 tbs. peanut butter

COCONUT DELIGHT

Serve with any tropical-island type bread which contains coconut. Also delicious with breads containing macadamia nuts. Heat first three ingredients over low heat until mixture thickens. Stir in coconut flakes until just mixed in and remove from heat. Serve warm. May be reheated in microwave. Makes ¾ cup.

½ cup coconut cream (canned)
¼ cup water

1½ tbs. cornstarch
1 tbs. coconut flakes

PAPAYA COCONUT

A tropical delight. Heat first four ingredients over low heat, stirring occasionally, until mixture thickens. Stir in coconut flakes until just mixed in and remove from heat. Serve warm. May be reheated in microwave. Makes ½ cup.

¼ cup papaya juice
¼ cup coconut cream (canned)
2 tbs. water

1 tbs. cornstarch
1 tbs. coconut flakes

PEACH AND ORANGE TOPPING

An astonishingly good topping or filling. May be made in advance and warmed for serving. Drain the peaches and process in blender or food processor until smooth. Combine all ingredients in a small saucepan and heat over low heat, stirring often, until sauce has thickened. Simmer until you are ready to serve or allow to cool and refrigerate until needed. Makes approximately 1 cup.

1 can (8¼ oz.) peaches, or pears
¼ cup orange juice
1 tbs. cornstarch

2 tbs. sugar
¼ tsp. cinnamon
⅛ tsp. grated orange peel

LEMON CREAM

This is absolutely out of this world. A "must try" with any lemon bread. Cream the softened cream cheese, add sugar and remaining ingredients until blended. Serve at room temperature or warmed in a microwave. Makes approximately ¾ cup.

4 oz. cream cheese, softened
¼ cup confectioners' sugar
1 tbs. lemon juice

½ tsp. grated lemon peel
1 tsp. poppy seeds, or to taste,
  optional

ORANGE FILLING

Any fruit concentrate or puree may be used in place of the orange concentrate. To puree fruits such as berries, simply process in a blender or food processor until the proper consistency is obtained.

	Small	Medium	Large
cream/yogurt cheese	4 oz.	6 oz.	8 oz.
powdered sugar	½ cup	¾ cup	1 cup
orange juice concentrate	1 to 2 tsp.	2 to 3 tsp.	1 to 1⅓ tbs.

CHEESE FILLING

Fill dough jelly-roll style for a quick and easy appetizer or meal.

	Small	Medium	Large
mozzarella cheese	½ cup	¾ cup	1 cup
ricotta cheese	½ cup	¾ cup	1 cup
egg	1	1½	2
garlic powder, optional	pinch	dash	⅛ tsp.
oregano	1 tbs.	1½ tbs.	2 tbs.

PRALINE ROLL FILLING

A delicious use of those southern pecans which should be finely ground in a food processor.

	Small	Medium	Large
melted butter	2 tbs.	3 tbs.	4 tbs.
pecans	½ cup	¾ cup	1 cup

ORANGE COCONUT

This is great with the coconut sweet dough or a basic sweet dough. Make as a jelly roll or rolled biscuits.

	Small	Medium	Large
orange/peach preserves	2 tbs.	3 tbs.	¼ cup
coconut flakes	2 tbs.	3 tbs.	¼ cup

CARAMEL FILLING I

Raisins could be added to this also — to taste.

	Small	Medium	Large
melted butter	2 tbs.	3 tbs.	4 tbs.
brown sugar	2 tbs.	3 tbs.	4 tbs.
chopped nuts	1/4 cup	1/3 cup	1/2 cup

CARAMEL FILLING II

Who can pass up a great caramel filling? Here's another variation.

	Small	Medium	Large
melted butter	2 tbs.	3 tbs.	4 tbs.
brown sugar	1/4 cup	6 tbs.	1/2 cup
light corn syrup	1 tbs.	1 1/2 tbs.	2 tbs.
finely chopped pecans	1/4 cup	1/3 cup	1/2 cup

SPINACH FILLING

*This is delicious paired with **Pizza Dough**, page 155, or **Spinach Dough**, page 153. Pair it with a salad or a bowl of soup for a satisfying lunch or supper.*

	Small	Medium	Large
chopped spinach	10 oz.	15 oz.	20 oz.
onion	2 to 3 tbs.	3 to 4 tbs.	4 to 6 tbs.
garlic clove, minced	1	1½	2
salt and lemon pepper	to taste	to taste	to taste
feta cheese, crumbled	1 cup	1½ cups	2 cups

Sauté onion and garlic in a little olive oil until soft and slightly golden. Spinach should be thawed and drained if frozen or washed and well drained if fresh. Add spinach, salt and pepper and simmer for about 5 minutes. Drain mixture and then toss in the cheese until well blended. Follow directions for stromboli, page 145.

Note: One box of frozen spinach is 10 oz.

SAUSAGE FILLING

*Use this filling with **Apple Dough**, page 152, for an unbeatable combination. If you prefer a really gooey, cheesy filling, the amount of cheese may be increased to taste.*

	Small	Medium	Large
sausage, diced	1 cup	1½ cups	2 cups
mozzarella cheese	½ cup	¾ cup	1 cup
rosemary	¼ tsp.	⅓ tsp.	½ tsp.
salt and pepper	to taste	to taste	to taste

To prepare filling, cook sliced or diced sausage and drain well. Mix filling ingredients together. Remove dough from machine and roll into 1 or 2 rectangles. Spread filling mixture on top of middle third of rectangle and fold each side over top of filling so that it is encased. Pinch ends closed and place fold side down on a well greased baking sheet. Rub top with a little olive oil and sprinkle rosemary on top as a garnish. Bake in a preheated 350° for 20 to 30 minutes or until golden brown.

SOURCES

Arrowhead Mills, Inc. (806) 346 0730
Box 2059
Hereford, TX 79045
   A wide variety of grains and flours. Health food store supplier and mail order catalog.

Bread Machine Newsletter
Donna R. German
976 Houston Northcutt Blvd., Suite 3
Mt. Pleasant, SC 29464
   Write for a complimentary review copy or with any questions you may have related to bread machine baking.

Cal-Gar Corp. (201) 692-2928
3 Fern Court
Flanders, NJ 07836
   Goldrush Sourdough Starters. Call to order or to locate where starters are sold near you.

Ener-G Foods (800) 331-5222
P. O. Box 84487
Seattle, WA 98124-5787
   Gluten free and allergy related items. Powdered egg replacer. Mail order catalog available.

Garden Spot Distributors (800) 829-5100
438 White Oak Road
New Holland, PA 17557
   Mail order of a wide variety of whole grains, flours, cereals, etc. Orders are shipped quickly and there are no added shipping charges except for pet foods.

Gibson's Healthful Living (800) 388-6844
570 South "G" Street
San Bernardino, CA 92498
   Mail order and store of whole grains and bread baking related items including bread machines and grain mills.

Great Valley Mills (215) 256-6648
687 Mill Road
Telford, PA 18969
   Mail order of stone ground flours, etc.

Jaffee Bros. Inc. (619) 749-1282
P. O. Box 636
Valley Center, CA 92082-0636
   Mail order of grains, flours and a wide variety of other food items.

K-Tec (800) 288-6455
370 E. 1300 S.
Orem, UT 84058
  Mail order of grain mill, grains, cereals and other bread baking related items.

King Arthur Flour (802) 649-3881
RR #2, Box 56
Norwich, VT 05055
  Mail order catalog of flours, grains, sourdough starter and many other bread baking related items including bulk yeast.

Mountain Woods (800) 835-0479
Box 65, Hwy 2 West
E. Glacier, Park, MT 59434
  Fiddle Bow Bread Knives

Walnut Acres (800) 433-3998
Penns Creek, PA 17862
  Mail order organic farm. Flours, grains, etc.

In addition to some of the mail order companies listed, yeast may be purchased in bulk through:

Fleischmann's Baker's Find (800)-966-2253

Red Star, mail only
Red Star
Consumer Service Dept.
433 E. Michigan Street
Milwaukee, WI 53202

For information on where to obtain bulk yeast sold in your area, call:

SAF - (800) 641-4615
Fermipan - (800)-662-4478

INDEX

SERVE CREATIVE, EASY, NUTRITIOUS MEALS WITH nitty gritty® COOKBOOKS

Entrées From Your Bread Machine
Muffins, Nut Breads and More
Healthy Snacks for Kids
100 Dynamite Desserts
Recipes for Yogurt Cheese
Sautés
Cooking in Porcelain
Appetizers
Recipes for the Loaf Pan
Casseroles
The Best Bagels are made at home*
   (*perfect for your bread machine)
The Toaster Oven Cookbook
Skewer Cooking on the Grill
Creative Mexican Cooking
Extra-Special Crockery Pot Recipes
Cooking in Clay
Marinades
Deep Fried Indulgences
Cooking with Parchment Paper
The Garlic Cookbook
Flatbreads From Around the World
From Your Ice Cream Maker

Favorite Cookie Recipes
Cappuccino/Espresso: The Book of
   Beverages
Indoor Grilling
Slow Cooking
The Best Pizza is made at home*
   (*perfect for your bread machine)
The Well Dressed Potato
Convection Oven Cookery
The Steamer Cookbook
The Pasta Machine Cookbook
The Versatile Rice Cooker
The Dehydrator Cookbook
The Bread Machine Cookbook
The Bread Machine Cookbook II
The Bread Machine Cookbook III
The Bread Machine Cookbook IV:
   Whole Grains and Natural Sugars
The Bread Machine Cookbook V:
   Favorite Recipes from 100 Kitchens
The Bread Machine Cookbook VI:
   *Hand-Shaped Breads from the
   Dough Cycle*

Worldwide Sourdoughs From Your
   Bread Machine
Recipes for the Pressure Cooker
The New Blender Book
The Sandwich Maker Cookbook
Waffles
The Coffee Book
The Juicer Book
The Juicer Book II
Bread Baking (traditional)
No Salt, No Sugar, No Fat Cookbook
Cooking for 1 or 2
Quick and Easy Pasta Recipes
The 9x13 Pan Cookbook
Low Fat American Favorites
Now That's Italian!
Low Salt, Low Sugar, Low Fat Desserts
Healthy Cooking on the Run
The Wok
Favorite Seafood Recipes
New International Fondue Cookbook

For a free catalog, write or call:
Bristol Publishing Enterprises, Inc.
P.O. Box 1737
San Leandro, CA 94577